THE CONVERSION OF
CONSTANTINE
AND PAGAN ROME

THE CONVERSION OF
CONSTANTINE
AND PAGAN ROME

BY
ANDREW ALFÖLDI

TRANSLATED BY
HAROLD MATTINGLY

OXFORD
AT THE CLARENDON PRESS

Oxford University Press, Great Clarendon Street, Oxford OX2 6DP
Oxford New York
Athens Auckland Bangkok Bogota Buenos Aires Calcutta
Cape Town Chennai Dar es Salaam Delhi Florence Hong Kong Istanbul
Karachi Kuala Lumpur Madrid Melbourne Mexico City Mumbai
Nairobi Paris São Paolo Singapore Taipei Tokyo Toronto Warsaw
and associated companies in
Berlin Ibadan

Oxford is a registered trade mark of Oxford University Press

Published in the United States by
Oxford University Press Inc., New York

© Oxford University Press 1948

Special edition for Sandpiper Books Ltd., 1998

British Library Cataloguing in Publication Data
Data available

ISBN 0-19-814356-7

1 3 5 7 9 10 8 6 4 2

Printed in Great Britain
on acid-free paper by
Bookcraft (Bath) Ltd.,
Midsomer Norton

FOREWORD

In 1937 I was able to demonstrate, by the publication of a series of documents, contemporary with the period and unquestionably authentic, that the reaction of the pagan Senate against the Christian Emperors, which culminated under Theodosius the Great, began at once after the victory won in the sign of Christ on the 28th of October A.D. 312. We already knew that it matured about the middle of the century; we see now that there was an even earlier phase. A second series of documents, which I edited in 1943, showed the continuation of that pagan movement in a camouflaged form after the defeat of Eugenius in A.D. 394 and its gradual decay in the course of the fifth century.

Such is the bare frame of the history of the national revival of the aristocracy of Rome. I was able to clothe it in flesh and blood by going over once again the literary and archaeological sources already known. It now appears that modern historians have made a mistake in treating Constantinople as the focus of the late Roman Empire in the fourth century and in neglecting the old capital. The Rome of that age still possessed great reserves of spiritual energy and, with them, the material resources to render its resistance to the new world of moral ideas effective. The struggle between the champions of the ethical and religious traditions of Rome and the leaders of the Christian movement thus acquires a unique historical significance.

This volume is the first of a series which I hope to write and the purpose of which will be to make these points clear. It aims at depicting the religious development of Constantine, that revolutionary in the purple, as it is mirrored in his fight with the only pagan group capable of resisting him. It is not based either on the one-sided Church sources or on the equally prejudiced views of modern rationalism. I present this study in almost exactly the form in which it appeared in a Hungarian review during the second World War, but with the addition of some bibliographical and critical notes.

The fresh evidence which opened my way to these new points

of view is supplied by coins, which hitherto have been unduly neglected or depreciated by modern scholars. The study of these coins has brought me into close contact with the English scholar who has been my friend and fellow worker for many years and has now willingly undertaken to translate my book into English. I am conscious how much I owe to his exact interpretation of my thought and to the dignity and clearness of his style.

The Secretary to the Delegates of the Clarendon Press and his staff have lent me their generous help and collaboration during publication; to them, as to my dear friend, Harold Mattingly, I offer my sincere thanks.

I offer this little volume in homage to another friend, Hugh Last, one of the lights of Oxford scholarship, who has been a tower of strength to me during a time of serious difficulty and whom I hold in high esteem not only as a scholar but as a man.

CONTENTS

INTRODUCTION

EVER since modern rationalism opened its campaign of 'enlightenment' against the Church, while the Church has reacted to its attacks with a vigorous defence, both parties have been trying, consciously or unconsciously, to fit the conversion of the first Christian Emperor into their own scheme and to interpret it accordingly. And what has been the result? The moderns have declined to reach their understanding of Constantine's fateful resolve from the conditions of late antiquity, from the spiritual state of the fourth century, from its proper environment, in fact. Generation after generation has shifted its valuation of that decisive step of Constantine, nay, more, of his whole life-work, to suit its own point of view, has involuntarily but relentlessly modernized it. Even to-day this procedure has not yet reached its end.[1]

The farthest departure from historical fact has, in my opinion, been achieved by those who have tried to obliterate the miracle of the *hoc signo victor eris* with the drastic thoroughness of the housewife, who used such a powerful acid to take the stain out of her son's coat that she destroyed the cloth as well. The champions of this view have not stopped with the miracle that took place in front of the Mulvian Bridge. With it they have discarded all the plain evidences of the religious fervour that brimmed the heart of Constantine, and have made of him a cynical figure, a divided and hypocritical personality who, only late and after long vacillation, placed himself on the Christian side. To justify this procedure all the elaborate resources of modern research have recently been applied. The impeccable documents, preserved in the contemporary Church historian, Eusebius, who from this point of view is entirely reliable, have been branded as forgeries. So, too, have the uniquely valuable deeds that relate to the sectarian movement of the Donatists in Africa. The Christian signs on the official coinage under Constantine have been disposed of by interpretation as ambiguous, if not actual pagan, symbols; or, alternatively, their evidence has been decried on the plea that they

[1] See Note 1, p. 124.

derive merely from the irresponsible initiative of subordinate officials. This method will not stand a serious test. It is not even, as we shall see, necessary for those who feel that the irrational element must be completely eliminated from the event in question. Authentic documents, and at least equally authentic, purely official, issues of coins supply us with absolute proof that the Emperor embraced the Christian cause with a suddenness that surprised all but his closest intimates. And, even though we may find that the famous vision was not enacted before the eyes of the whole world but only in the Emperor's dream, it was an experience real to him, which had historical effects of world-wide importance. To try to minimize or cancel its significance is labour lost.

There are many causes in men's own minds that have hindered a right appraisal of Constantine, or have, at the least, given rise to perverse and unjustifiable conceptions of him. But there is also an external cause that has confused judgement on the matter. If you look back on the figure of the Emperor from the Middle Ages and observe how his activities prescribed the fortunes of the Byzantine world for centuries ahead, you get the impression that these vast effects were due to the achievement of a single man, with no historical introduction, no organic development behind him. Seen thus, Constantine is like a mighty rock, jutting skyward out of the sea of history. But if, on the other hand, you begin with the Early Empire and view the course of evolution in the most diverse departments of life from that angle, if you see that evolution, however varied the forms it takes, always describing the same upward and downward curve, you are left without any doubt that every step taken by Constantine simply supplied a reasonable solution to problems already existing and just grown ripe for settlement ; and that those steps must have been taken by the occupants of the throne—perhaps decades later, perhaps in somewhat different form—but taken without fail.

For those rulers of nations who have exercised a decisive influence on the shaping of human destinies have certainly not been all men of a single kind. One you find raised to the dizzy height of a throne by his own authentic greatness. Another gains recognition by the sheer weight of his rude, barbarian energies. Many have simply been lifted on the tides of mass emotion or brought to the helm of State at the critical moment by other circumstances, outside their control. Such men have had no more difficulty in discharging their role in history than those high-born ladies who have only to press a trembling finger on a button for the iron colossus of a battleship to glide smoothly into the sea.

Constantine, indeed, was not privileged to pluck his laurels so easily. There had already been one Emperor before him who had determined for centuries in advance the path that the Roman Empire was to tread, the Emperor Augustus. Just as Constantine had had his mighty forerunner in the person of Diocletian, so too, as we all know, Julius Caesar had smoothed the way for the constitutional reforms of Augustus. Augustus, like Constantine, if we look back on his reign from the vantage-point of after-ages, appears to us as the man who held the initiative at every point in the reform of State and society. And yet, in his case, too, it becomes clear, as we test what lay behind his activities, that his lofty conception of the Principate had already been sketched out for him by Cicero; clear, too, that he was only able to give a lasting shape to the Roman Empire because a mighty historical development had just reached maturity. But despite these striking parallels, Constantine is left far behind by Augustus. Look at the brilliant imitative art of the talented Claudius Claudianus—how it pales before the unique, unspoiled Roman gift of Virgil! Look, again, at the organic modelling, the delicate individualization of the portraits of the Augustan age—how they throw into the shade, from the point of view of creative art, the grandiose but mechanical head of Constantine on his Basilica in Rome! What a distance separates the artistic refinements of an Arretine pot of the Augustan age from the rough, though decorative, figures of an African pot of the fourth century! Just the same distance is to be seen between the value of the achievements of the two Emperors. What Constantine achieved might, under favourable circumstances, have been accomplished—and with more tact—by the highly gifted, much traduced, Gallienus. Even the coarse but worthy and consistent Aurelian was equal to such tasks. But the work of

Augustus was the unique creation of a superior spirit, and it could never be repeated.

It cannot be our aim to record the many mutually exclusive conceptions that have been formed of the Emperor who first inscribed the name of Christ on his banner. Enough if we realize that research in the last three centuries has, for all its contradictions and controversies, achieved immense progress. The old familiar sources have been thoroughly scoured, new sources have been discovered and made available for study; scholars of the most diverse schools have contributed valuable observations and results that will stand. Wide perspectives have been opening out before us. We have already to hand a considerable number of pieces of many-coloured mosaic. If, after a careful sorting, we can add a few new stones and put them all back, without prejudice, in their right, original places, the genuine character of the victory of Christ is bound to appear. Our reconstruction will not, indeed, involve any sensational reversal of earlier results, but it will yield something important enough. It will show us how the Christianization of the Empire gave rise to a violent reaction on the part of those who carried the national tradition of Rome. It will make the immense scope and historical significance of that reaction for the first time fully intelligible.

I
THE ANTECEDENTS OF THE CONVERSION OF CONSTANTINE

ABOUT the year A.D. 300, when Constantine was in his early manhood and when his view of life had begun to take a clear shape, the religions of the ancient world were already in decay, and only a few august deities retained their power of attraction. But the religious sense, far from fading with the old gods, had actually increased in strength to an amazing degree. It filled both the lowest practices of superstition and the refined conceptions of monotheism with a new and unheard-of potency that was to make history. The spiritual life of the cultured circles, the animal existence of the most backward strata of the population were alike filled and directed by religious fervour.

That general process of unification that was then taking place in all fields of life did not leave untouched the polytheistic religions. In the melting-pot monotheism began to crystallize out around two resistant nuclei. The first of these was the worship of the Sun-god. Philosophy changing into theosophy, the astrological speculations of the Chaldeans, the wild mysticism of the half-Christian Gnostics met here in one wild confusion; and with them met that religion of the Sun that pervaded the whole East and the primitive ideas of the Indo-Germans and their like about the magical power and omnipotence of the god. This deification of the Sun, in this composite form, was vastly attractive. Official Roman policy had once ventured in this direction and had tried to exalt 'Sol Invictus' as *dominus imperii Romani* to be the heavenly lord of the Roman Empire.[1] The second nucleus of crystallization was, of course, the Church. At first both of these had had their influence on Constantine. From the time when he was first able to develop an independent policy—in the years before the overthrow of Maxentius—the Sun-god came to the front, beside Mars, on his Gallic coinage.[2] When Constantine in

[1] See Note 2, p. 124.
[2] J. Maurice, *Numismatique Constantinienne*, ii, 1911, xx ff.

A.D. 310 dedicated rich gifts in a shrine of Apollo in Gaul, it was probably for the universal Sol-Apollo, not for any local Gallic deity, that they were intended.[1] Constantine, even after the victory that he had won by the aid of the Redeemer, did not at once break the ties that bound him to the invincible Sun. Modern research has even ventured, on these grounds, to question the fact of the conversion of Constantine, or at least its sincerity. But this ambiguity in his conduct is astonishing only to us. In the world as seen in that religious chaos, such a confusion was quite easy to understand, and the most varied justifications could be found for it.[2] What, in my view, is really remarkable and astonishing is the fact that Constantine succeeded, in one short decade, in shedding his last vestiges of polytheism.

From the autumn of A.D. 312 the attractions of the Sun-god in Constantine's world of thought were steadily on the decline. But his old sympathy for the Church of Christ grew correspondingly stronger. He had inherited this understanding for Christianity from his father. Bloody persecutions of the Christians had been set on foot and pursued for years with relentless rigour by the colleagues of Constantius. But Constantius himself had been reluctant to begin them in his own Western section of the Empire and had been lukewarm in carrying them out. Belief in Christ had already struck root in the family of Constantine.[3] This surprising fact is betrayed by the Christian name of one of Constantius Chlorus' daughters, Anastasia.[4] Our Emperor himself declared, at a later date, that his father had been a deeply religious man and had always

---

[1] *Incerti paneg. Constantino Aug. d.* 21. 3 and 7 (pp. 217 ff. Guil. Behrens).

[2] Cf. the excellent remarks of L. Salvatorelli, *Ricerche religiose*, iv, 1928, 303 f.

[3] G. Boissier, *La Fin du paganisme*, i[8]. 14 f.; O. Seeck, *Geschichte des Unterganges der antiken Welt*, i[4], 1921, 61 f. and 475; L. Salvatorelli, *Ricerche religiose*, iv, 1928, 292 f.; R. Andreotti, *Didaskaleion*, N.S. ix, 1930, fasc. 1. 157 ff., fasc. 2. 1 ff., &c.

[4] L. Duchesne, *Histoire ancienne de l'Église*, ii[2], 1907, 57; H. Lietzmann, *Sitzungsberichte der Preuss. Akad., phil.-hist. Kl.*, 1937, 268; id., *Geschichte der alten Kirche*, iii, 1938, 144; H. v. Schoenebeck, 'Beiträge zur Religionspolitik des Maxentius und Konstantin', *Klio*, Beiheft xliii, 1939, 73, note 1. For a rather different view cf. A. Piganiol, *L'Empereur Constantin*, 1932, 34.

Conversion of Constantine 7

called on the Redeemer for aid.[1] This can hardly be a mere invention. Apart from these impressions derived from his father's house, Constantine seems to have found something to draw him closer to the oppressed Christians in the hatred that he felt for Diocletian and Galerius, the authors of the persecutions. They had excluded him from the succession to the imperial College of Four and had thus offended his boundless passion for recognition. The bitterness of his feelings for them found public expression later in an edict in which, for all to hear, he reviled them for their bloody persecutions of the Church.[2] This public insult to Emperors of high renown, not long since dead, was a revolutionary utterance to come from the occupant of the throne. It was something unheard of in that Roman world that was lost in admiration of antiquity and that regarded the defence of the good old morality as its supreme duty. That Constantine's revulsion from the Roman past did not begin with the edict that we have just mentioned, but was already complete in his youth, is beyond all possible doubt.[3] But there were other reasons, of a positive character, for his turning towards Christianity.

According to his Christian biographer, it is true, the conversion of Constantine was sudden, without any warning. This is a feature of the miracle story as a literary genre. The surprising turn of events, brought about by a Higher Power, is normally represented in as incomprehensible a form as possible.[4] 'But',

[1] Euseb. *Vita Const.* 2. 49; cf. 1. 27.
[2] Ibid. 2. 51; 43. 53. It is these outbreaks of passion that represent his real emotions, not the coin-types, on which, to emphasize his legitimacy, he still has Maximianus Herculius shown as late as A.D. 314 and 324. See O. Voetter, 'Die Ahnenmünzen Kaiser Constantins des Grossen', *Separat-Abdruck aus den Mittheilungen des Clubs der Münz- u. Medaillenfreunde in Wien*, 1895.
[3] On these problems, cf. Th. Keim, *Der Übertritt Konstantins zum Christentum*, 1862, 42 ff., 94 ff.; V. Duruy, *Histoire des Romains*, vii², 1885, 135 ff.; G. Boissier, op. cit. i⁸. 16; F. X. Funk, *Kirchengeschichtliche Abhandlungen und Untersuchungen*, 1899, 15 ff.; E. Caspar, *Geschichte des Papsttums*, i, 1930, 107; A. Piganiol, op. cit. 36 ff., &c.
[4] This idea has made its way into the most recent literature: 'He yielded to a sudden impulse, call it pathological or inspired, as you will', writes, for example, F. Lot, *La Fin du monde antique*, 1927, 351.

writes Mgr. Duchesne,[1] 'it is very hard to admit that Constantine had till then had absolutely no knowledge of Christianity. His biography, at this point, betrays something very like deliberate trickery.' But the idea was no invention of Eusebius; it is due to the religious fervour of the Emperor himself— that Emperor who, two years after he had inscribed the name of Christ on his banner, wrote to the Synod of Arles in terms like these:[2]

'The inconceivable goodness of our God forbids that mankind should continue to wander in the dark. . . . I have realized this truth from many examples outside myself, but I can also confirm it from my own experience. There were things in my own nature that were devoid of righteousness and I seemed to see no heavenly power that I might have been carrying hidden in my breast. . . . But Almighty God, who watches from the high tower of Heaven, has vouchsafed to me what I have not deserved. Verily past number are the blessings that He, in His heavenly goodness, has bestowed on me, His servant.'

He can write thus, although he had never been an unbeliever. Ten years later he is again goaded by his religious zeal into a betrayal of his feelings. 'Long ago, even from the beginning, it was clear to any who could form a right and reasonable judgement of the Almighty, to what great advantage the careful maintenance of the holy Christian worship contrasted with those who tried to oppose and degrade it.'[3] We have no reason, therefore, to doubt what Lactantius wrote only a few years after Constantine came to the throne. 'Having attained Empire, Constantine, the Augustus, first restored to the Christians the free exercise of their religion and their God; and to confirm the restoration of the holy religion was his first act.'[4] We cannot admit that this was merely a move in the political game of chess.[5] Constantine's behaviour

[1] L. Duchesne, *Histoire ancienne de l'Église*, ii², 1907, 59.

[2] See Note 3, p. 124.

[3] Euseb. *Vita Const.* 2. 24, p. 51, Heikel; cf. 2. 49 and 52. 55, end. G. Pasquali, *Hermes*, 1910, 376, has shown that Eusebius had already given an extract of this edict in Chapter 20 f.; but we must not assume, because of this carelessness in editing, that the complete text was added by someone else.

[4] Lactant. *De mortibus persecutorum*, 24. 9; id. *Instit. divin.* i. 1. 13. Cf. L. Salvatorelli, *Ricerche religiose*, iv, 1928, 295 ff.

[5] As Ed. Schwartz supposes, *Göttinger gel. Nachrichten*, 1904, 520.

in the years that followed makes it plain why in A.D. 310 he suspended those persecutions in which his father had only reluctantly shared. It was because of his belief in the power of the Redeemer. In the other sections of the Empire the hand of the State still pressed heavily on the Church. Maxentius, the ruler of Italy and North Africa, was the only one to join Constantine in abandoning the policy of bloody suppression, and he was not recognized by the imperial college. Only once did he take severe measures—against the riots that broke out at a papal election.[1] Apart from that he actually showed favour to the Church; in A.D. 311 he allowed it to resume its landed property.[2]

In the rest of the Empire, too, the attempt to wipe out the Faithful broke down; it broke on the heroic resistance of the *élite* and on the perfect functioning of the social and political organization of the Church, even in face of the severest difficulties. In A.D. 311 the Emperor Galerius, the instigator of the persecutions, felt himself compelled to acknowledge the futility of bloodshed, while still absolutely declining to give up his essential point of view. His edict of toleration was revolutionary in its implications. The confessors came back to their jubilant brethren from prison, from exile and forced labour, flushed with victory, dumbfounding friend and foe alike with the still fresh marks of their sufferings and of the pains that they had overcome. The Church buildings rose from their ruins before the eyes of the pagans.[3]

Galerius himself, then, by his edict of toleration, admitted the complete failure of the campaign of destruction, even though with gnashing of teeth. What a blow this meant for the earlier policy traditionally pursued towards the Christians has already been duly emphasized by my predecessors.[4] What the

---

[1] Lactant., op. cit. 15. 7.
[2] E. Groag, *Realenc. d. class. Altertumswiss.*, abbreviated in *RE.* xiv. 2462 ff.; E. Caspar, op. cit. 101; H. v. Schoenebeck, op. cit. 13 f.
[3] Lactant. *De mort. pers.* 35. 2; Euseb. *H.E.* ix. 1. 7 ff.
[4] Th. Zahn, *Constantin d. Gr. u. die Kirche*, 1876, 11 f.; V. Schultze, *Geschichte des Untergangs des griechisch-römischen Heidentums*, i, 1887, 29; R. Mariano, *Nuova antologia*, ser. 3, xxvii, 1890, 278; A. Manaresi, *L'impero*

Roman Empire now gave up was nothing less than the procedure that had been normal with its magistrates for centuries.
They had required men to prove and express their loyalty by
the performance of acts of sacrifice to the gods and the supreme
ruler of the State; this was bound to be a stumbling-block to
the Christians, who could not sacrifice to strange gods. That
was why the compulsion to sacrifice could be used with such
success in the persecutions as a touchstone of Christian sentiment. All this was now past. The State found itself compelled
to adopt the position that the Church had taken from the
outset. The political reliability of the Faithful could now be
attested to everybody's satisfaction by the simple prayer for
the head of the State, for the ruling classes, and for the subjects
of the Empire.[1]

The Christian movement, at once a religion and a social and
political organization, had already struck its roots deep in all
provinces of the Empire.[2] Now, as a result of the events we
have described, it finally burst the bounds that had confined
it.[3] 'The burning question of the century confronted the
Emperor with a more imperative demand for solution than
ever.'[4] Quite apart from this special case, questions of religious
policy stood in the foreground of public interest. As we all
know, the spiritual justification of the Empire, as an organization, had in the course of ages assumed different forms.
Broadly speaking, we may say that the Empire of the first
century after Christ was founded on a purely political conception and bore a Roman stamp. In the second century it had
a moral and philosophical base and a Greek tone. Finally, in
the third century it justified its existence on religious grounds
and bore the hall-mark of the hellenized East.[5] That moderate

romano e il cristianesimo, 1914, 481 ff.; K. Bihlmeyer, *Theolog. Quartalschrift*,
xciv, 1912, 411 ff., 527; J. Geffcken, *Der Ausgang des griechisch-römischen
Heidentums*, 1920, 91; J. R. Knipfing, *Revue Belge de philologie et d'hist.* i,
1922, 693 ff., &c.

[1] A. Alföldi, *Klio*, xxxi, 1938, 323 ff.; id. *Pisciculi*, 1939, 1 ff.
[2] See Note 4, p. 124.
[3] So, for example, A. Manaresi, op. cit. 482.
[4] V. Schultze, op. cit.
[5] R. Laqueur, *Probleme der Spätantike*, 1930, 3 ff., with a slightly different
characterization of the third stage.

monarchy of the early period which we call the 'Principate' had a legal structure and a basis in fact; but the later Roman absolutism, which we call the 'Dominate', was based on the sense of reverence in men's minds.

As early as the second century we find a conception of the Emperor gaining ground which insisted that prosperity in peace and victory in war alike were not guaranteed by the individual qualities of the Emperor, but were the gift of some particular deity, who thus rewarded devotion to his service. It is no longer powerful initiative and courage, intellectual gifts and attainments, but the strict observance of religious duties that becomes increasingly important in the occupant of the throne.[1] The host of ancient gods were becoming confused with one another, and, in this process of intermixture, ever new deities would rise into prominence and take the centre of the stage. It became necessary, therefore, as new divinities from time to time established their supremacy, to claim them as protectors of the throne, until finally monotheism was established and, on its way to triumph, narrowed down more and more the circle of gods to choose from. By the year A.D. 270 the unification of the polytheistic conceptions of God had already gone a long way. Aurelian could think seriously of raising the general conception of the Sun-god as *Sol dominus imperii Romani* to the post of supreme deity of the Empire. The relation of throne and altar had already become quite intimate. The division of the Empire into four sections by Diocletian required four divine patrons for the four rulers; but the principle of the connexion of each individual ruler with his own divine protector was not thereby obscured. The restoration of the unity of the Empire, on the other hand, led inevitably to the belief that a single divine power must watch over the single earthly ruler.[2] Constantine, of course, could not grasp these tendencies and the inevitable results of their evolution along the line of historical development, but, with acute political instinct, he accurately diagnosed the situation

[1] See Note 5, p. 125.
[2] A. Alföldi, '25. Jahre Römisch-Germanische Kommission', *Vortrag*, 9 Dec. 1927, 1929, 19 ff.; W. Weber, *Probleme der Spätantike*, 1930, 87 ff.; A. Alföldi, *Pisciculi*, 12 ff.

that had arisen out of that development and that was now ripe for solution. It makes no difference to the importance of his decision whether he was directed by the wise judgement of an historian or the acumen of a statesman.

The Church, for its part, was not nearly so unimportant, politically, as to require no respect—though this has often been assumed.[1] On the contrary, it was ripe to take over the role of leadership in the ancient world.[2] Its basic doctrine of the One and Only God was not so far removed from that idea of one supreme God that was developing out of the confusion of religions. The moral demands of Christianity and its teaching of redemption show a close relationship to the ideals of the highest classes of educated pagans. Christian theology, no less than the thought of the spiritual aristocracy that worshipped one supreme Being, was built up out of the resources of Greek philosophy. The forms of Christian worship reveal frequent correspondences to the sacred acts of the mystery religions. In the sacred buildings of Christians and pagans alike ancient art supplied the means of expression whereby reverence might be evoked and the Divine idea glorified.

But, despite all these agreements, the monotheism of the Christian Church was far more original and pure than the deism of its rivals. In its teaching, it was not only chosen spirits that might hope to be raised up to the throne of God. The simplest man, devoid of any culture, might reach that high goal by personal experience of the story of redemption. This experience of the Christian life clothes the longing for purification and the ideal of eternal life in far higher forms than the kindred spiritual strivings of the pagans. The divine men of paganism are no more than pale copies, inferior imitations of Christ. We see, then, that paganism was already sailing in the wake of the Church. Its world of spirit was already in decay and was bound, sooner or later, to fail before its rival.

From this point of view, it is of some importance to note that the pagan cults were nothing but a confused medley, very loosely bound together by the customary dedications to 'all

---

[1] For example, O. Seeck, *Geschichte des Untergangs der antiken Welt*, i[4]. 59 f.

[2] The following sketch depends on the line of thought of K. Müller, *Kirchengeschichte*, i[2], 1929, 344 f.

the gods'. They had no common organization and tended to break up into their atoms. Vain were all attempts to force this chaos into a system of theology and give it organic form. The Church, on the other hand, with its complete unity, with its claim to total rule, demanded the exclusive allegiance of all its members. For this faultless religious unity was welded together by a first-rate social organization—a Socialist organization, in the modern sense of the words—and it was all based on the inner fraternity, derived from a purified love of humanity, unknown before.

Yet, closely as the organization of the Church agrees with the Socialist movement of the nineteenth century, its attitude to the State was quite a different one.[1] It has no desire to overthrow the Empire, it does not preach hatred and battle against those strata of society on which the State rests; and, even in the midst of persecution, it tries to remain loyal and faithful. How could Constantine fail to see the advantages of this unique organization, which had emerged victorious, nay, with strength renewed, out of the violent and terrifying attempts of the powers of the State under Decius, Diocletian, and Galerius to suppress it ? A modern statesman, in the place of Constantine, would have thought of a political alliance with the priesthood. But the men of that age saw in the limitless attractiveness of the Christian community the direct agency of God ; and the written utterances of Constantine mirror that same naïvety of conception that animated his contemporaries. That was why Constantine did not conclude any alliance with the community on earth, but placed himself under the protection of the God, who had given His Faithful such vast powers of resistance.

When Constantine, spurred on by his boundless lust for power,[2] set his Gallic army in motion, to win him the rule of Italy, he had, according to the testimony of Eusebius,[3] bishops

---

[1] This parallel was developed up to a point by L. M. Hartmann, *Christentum und Sozialismus*[3], 1916. Cf. my comments in '25. Jahre Römisch-Germanische Kommission', 1929, 18, note 53.

[2] Ed. Schwartz, *Göttinger gel. Nachrichten*, 1904, 525, 526, note 1; E. Groag, *RE*. xiv. 2471 f.

[3] Euseb. *Vita Const.* i. 32.

in his entourage. After his triumphant entry into Rome on the 29th of October A.D. 312 we find Bishop Ossius of Corduba at his side ;[1] from now on he remains the confidant and favourite of the Emperor. Ossius, then, had accompanied him from Gaul to Rome. That he already played no slight role among his followers is shown by the official mission with which he was entrusted, immediately after the overthrow of Maxentius, in connexion with Constantine's measures to settle the dispute with the Donatists in North Africa. It cannot be doubted that this man, of whom unfortunately we know very little and whose writings are lost, exercised no slight influence on Constantine just when, before the battle of the Mulvian Bridge, he was toying with the idea of crossing over to the side of Christ. The imperial favour which surrounded Ossius may even have been the reward for his good counsels. On his later campaigns, too, Constantine took with him priests, to lend him the support of their prayers in battle. Ossius will, certainly, not have failed in the like service. But far more important, it seems, were his quiet conversations with the Emperor. In the course of them Constantine's resolve to implore the aid of Christ—and, if He assisted him, to give himself completely to His cause, grew to maturity. Perhaps it was just these confidential talks with Ossius that determined the exact forms and conditions under which Constantine confided himself to the Redeemer.

All that we know of the development of the youthful Constantine shows that his decisive step had many preparatory stages and a long history behind it. There is, therefore, no validity in those ingenious combinations that represent the great resolve as a move suggested by the political situation of the moment or as a dramatic decision, suddenly brought about by the excited condition of his nerves on the eve of the fateful battle. It is equally evident that the divine intervention cannot have been as unexpected as Constantine himself after-

---

[1] Attention to this important fact has been called by O. Seeck, *Gesch. d. Untergangs d. antiken Welt*, i⁴. 495, basing himself on the passage in Eusebius, *H.E.* x. 6. 2: 'As his Bishopric was in the Gallic section of the Empire and he can hardly have been in the domains of Maxentius during the war, it is more than probable that he came to the Capital with Constantine's army.'

wards asserted and as his Christian biographer later embroidered the theme. We have already seen how this idea
sprang from the lively imagination of the Apostle in the purple,
who proclaimed the mighty event in his own spiritual history
in the style of the divine revelations. There were not a few
works of religious propaganda, passing from hand to hand at
the time, which showed how the angel of the Almighty chose
out this man or that and gave him power over the secret forces
of the creation, and how the new prophet then proceeded to
publish his story abroad and endeavour to convert the world.[1]
Just such an impression was made on Constantine by that
experience that determined for the whole of his future the
direction that his activities were to take.

[1] For example, the anonymous prophet in Poimandres, *Corp. Hermet.* i. 26.

II

THE VISION OF CONSTANTINE

MOST of us are familiar with the account given by Eusebius, Bishop of Caesarea, of the conversion of Constantine a quarter of a century after the event. According to his account the Almighty gave ear to Constantine's fervent prayer and sent him a divine sign of wonder in the sky. Above the setting sun the Emperor, and his army with him, saw the sign of the Cross, outlined in rays of light, and, with it, the words: 'In this sign thou shalt conquer.' He did not at first understand the vision —so he maintained on oath to Eusebius—until Christ appeared to him in a dream and commanded him to copy the sign that he had seen in the sky and use it in battle as a talisman of defence.[1] Constantine obeyed and ordered that a standard made of gold and studded with sparkling jewels[2] should be prepared, to bring salvation and protect from harm. Henceforward it was borne at the head of all his armies. He likewise caused the initial letters of the Redeemer's name to be set on his helmet and continued to bear them there. Deeply impressed by the wonder that he had seen, Constantine summoned Christian priests to him. They taught him about Christ and explained that the Cross was the symbol of victory over death. Convinced by their interpretation of the miracle that a divine revelation had indeed been vouchsafed to him, Constantine became anxious to occupy himself with the reading of Holy Writ and, by every means in his power, to serve the God whom he had beheld. It was full of good hope, then, that he went into battle against the blood-stained and dissolute tyrant.[3] In reliance on the help of God he gained victory after victory. And, as once the Lord, to protect Moses and his God-fearing people, had cast Pharaoh and his war-chariots and the might of his army into the sea, and had sunk his chosen leaders in the Red Sea, so now Maxentius with his bodyguard sank 'in the deeps like a stone' when, fleeing before the might of the God

---

[1] Euseb. *Vita Const.* 1. 28–9. Greek, τούτῳ νίκα; Latin, hoc signo victor eris.　　　　　　[2] Ibid. 31.　　　　　　[3] Ibid. 32.

who fought for Constantine, he tried to escape over the bridge of boats.[1] The jubilant song of the soldiers rose sky-high.

Towards the close of his life, when his whole being was flooded with religious enthusiasm, Constantine represented all these events as a succession of miracles, following on the revelation vouchsafed him—just as though there had been no bloody slaughters for him to execute, but he had simply made a pilgrimage in which faith worked the wonders. The pompous and exaggerated style of Eusebius gives it away. The historian doubtless contributed the fine flowers of his own piety to adorn the story as heard from the Emperor. But, objectively regarded, the course of events was much more commonplace, more true to normal human experience, than that edifying story in all its dazzling colours.[2] But it was no whit less important in its consequences.

Not that Eusebius' account has no kernel of historical fact. We can prove beyond a doubt, by the evidence of coin-types appearing soon after, that Constantine caused the monogram of Christ to be inscribed on his helmet before the decisive battle with Maxentius. Again, it is an assured fact that the banner with the sign of Christ became the sacred ensign of the armies of Constantine and, afterwards, of the Christian Empire in general.[3] But a comparison of the description of Eusebius with the rest of the evidence shows that it is marred by one particular misunderstanding, which is quite easy to explain.[4] It was not the Cross that appeared in the vision, but the monogram of Christ, consisting of the letters Chi Rho. A much

---

[1] Ibid. 37–8; cf. 39.

[2] For the details, see my article, 'Hoc signo victor eris', in *Pisciculi*, 1939, 1 ff. The arguments of H. Grégoire, *Byzantion*, xiv, 1939, 350 ff., have not given me any fresh reason for changing my position; see W. Ensslin, *Klio*, xxxiii, 1941, 358, and J. Vogt, *Zeitschr. f. Kirchengesch.* 1942, 17 ff.

[3] There is an anachronism in the description of the *labarum* in Eusebius. The heads of the Caesars, the sons of Constantine, are painted with his on the flag; and this, of course, is impossible before the nomination of the Caesars. Later, without any doubt, the portraits of the young colleagues were placed on the ensign of Christ. This lapse of memory on the part of the Church historian in no way deprives the rest of his description of its value.

[4] See my article, quoted above; Eusebius' error had already been detected by G. Costa, *Religione e politica nell' impero romano*, 1923, 245 ff.

better attested version of the vision which partly completes, partly corrects, that of Eusebius is found in Lactantius, the Christian rhetorician who, not long after these events, became the tutor of the eldest son of Constantine and wrote his pamphlet on the 'Deaths of the Persecutors'. In his account the wonder did not take place anywhere in Gaul or in broad daylight, but immediately before the battle of the Mulvian Bridge. The Emperor, in a dream, saw the initial letters of the name of Christ and the words of light, *Hoc signo victor eris*.[1] Further, we are told, Christ instructed Constantine not only to bear the sign of wonder on his helmet, but also to have it painted on the shields of his soldiers.[2] According to Lactantius, the sign was represented by a vertical stroke, rounded at the top, drawn through the middle of the Chi. We must interpret this to mean that the Rho, hastily painted on the shields, took the form of a round-headed pin. How exact this observation is is proved by the precisely similar variation of the monogram on a coin-type, issued about A.D. 320 in many mints, on instructions from headquarters.

The divine announcement—'In this sign thou shalt conquer'—is an historical fact, then, seen though it was only in a dream. That it was an overwhelming experience, not an ingenious invention to cheat the masses, is proved beyond a doubt by the over-mastering enthusiasm with which Constantine ever afterwards fought for the cause of Christ and His Church.[3]

It was not merely nervous excitability before the decisive battle that made Constantine receptive to visions. We know that he experienced divine instruction in dreams on other

[1] A coin struck in A.D. 350 proves that this is the correct form of the words that Constantine saw blazing in the sky, and not the *in hoc signo vinces*, which is a modern translation back from the Greek, τούτῳ νίκα, of Eusebius.

[2] Lactant. *De mort. pers.* 44. 5–6.

[3] H. Grégoire and other scholars, following him, have tried to represent this as an imitation of a pagan vision seen in Gaul, which is mentioned in a Panegyrist. But J. Bidez, *L'Antiquité class.* i, 1932, 5 ff., has already seen that the vision of Apollo only took place in the fancy of the Panegyrist and is a mere literary fiction. Cf. also H. Lietzmann, *Sitzungsberichte der Preuss. Akad., phil.-hist. Kl.*, 1937, 264 ff.

occasions when he had important decisions to make.[1] He
himself referred the foundation of his new capital to a suggestion of this kind from heaven. Nor was he alone in his age in
believing that the heavenly powers are wont to use this means
of directing men how they shall act. Countless votive offerings
still record how their givers did this or that on divine instruction, received in a dream. Even in the works of Porphyrius,
the greatest philosopher of the age, we often encounter kindly
spirits and evil demons who guide the life of mortals by visions.
This particular Neoplatonist even imagined that the spirits
could be invoked and exorcized by art.[2] The leading classes
of Christians of the day—Lactantius himself is an example—
shared in this conviction; only they expected the supernatural
results, not from the conjuration of gods and demons, but from
the utterance or showing of the name of Christ and the use of
the symbol of the Cross. As the conviction that the gods give
such warnings in sleep was so widespread, the fulfilment of the
vision that came to Constantine in sleep must have made a
deep impression on every hand.[3] The Emperor Licinius,
brother-in-law of Constantine, himself tried to trade on this
psychological motif, and gave out that he too had had a vision,
promising him the victory, when he was about to settle
accounts with Maximin Daza. Lactantius, when he wrote,
believed that Licinius had had his own enlightenment from on
high.[4] But, before long, it proved that the Christian colouring
of the religion of Licinius was mere accident and hypocrisy.

It is clear from what we have been saying that the ideas
and inferences associated with the vision of Constantine were
nothing but abortions of the excitable religious fancy of the
late Roman Empire. Constantine was prevented from breaking
away from this debased form of religion by his inferior education. Some scholars, indeed, suppose him to have grown up in

[1] Sozom. *H.E.* ii. 3. 3; Theophan. *Chronogr.*, anno mundi, 5816; *Cod.
Theod.* xiii. 5. 7, and, commenting on it, O. Seeck, op. cit. i[4]. 473; iii[2]. 559;
H. Lietzmann, *Geschichte der alten Kirche*, iii, 1938, 135, note 1.
[2] See L. Salvatorelli, *Ricerche religiose*, iv, 1928, 305. Julian the Apostate,
too, was full of such ideas; cf., for example, G. Boissier, op. cit. i[8]. 115. My
intended volume on Valentinian is to contain fuller details.
[3] See Note 6, p. 125.
[4] Lactant. *De mort. pers.* 46. 2.

the atmosphere of the palace and to have realized, from the first, the importance of thorough and individual education of the personality.[1] But such was not the case. The rough, good-tempered Illyrian soldier in whose house Constantine grew up had laid little stress on letting his son have a good education; what he wanted above all was to make him a good general and efficient administrator. At the most, we may allow that Constantine acquired in the air of a palace decent principles of respect for culture, and that this spurred him on to let his own sons have a really thorough classical education.

For all his high birth Constantine was certainly not well educated; he was *litteris minus instructus*, to quote the words of a reliable authority.[2] A letter of his, it is true, survives, written in beautifully smooth and resonant phrases, which show off the perfect literary education of its composer;[3] but that only makes it the plainer that the brilliant stylist was not the Emperor, who signed it, but a man of letters in the imperial chancellory. What Constantine actually composed himself—letters discussing Christian doctrine and the like—are ponderous and wordy, long-winded compilations. A similar clumsiness and unbridled passion is revealed in his legislation.[4]

If Constantine's acquaintance with worldly literature was slight, his knowledge of the Bible was equally weak.[5] The subtle speculations of theology were a closed book to him. A distinguished modern Church historian has branded his letter to Bishops Alexander and Arius as a forgery, because he was scared by the pieces of 'childish silliness' that occur in it.[6] But such primitive ideas characterize the whole of Constantine's religious writings and betray thereby their imperial composi-

[1] R. Laqueur, *Probleme der Spätantike*, 1930, 7. Aur. Victor, *Caes.* 40. 12 is a piece of empty flattery addressed to the son of Constantine.

[2] *Origo Constantini Aug.* 2 (*Mon. Germ. Hist., auct. ant.* ix, p. 7).

[3] *Publili Optatiani Porfyrii carm.*, ed. E. Kluge, pp. 39 ff.

[4] E. Kornemann, *Römische Geschichte*, ii, 1939, 433.

[5] I. Heikel, *Eusebius Werke*, i, p. lxxxix; L. Wrzoł, *Weidenauer Studien*, i, 1906, 253 ff.

[6] P. Batiffol, *La Paix Constantinienne*³, 1914, 315 f. Against his view, see A. v. Harnack, *Dogmengeschichte*, ii⁴, 1924, 194; Ed. Schwartz, *Gött. gel. Nachr.* 1905, 288 f.

tion.[1] Proud as Constantine may have been of his wisdom, derived from Smaller Catechisms, loud as may have been the praises of his courtiers for his zealous declaration of faith, thorough as may have been the process of 'combing out' to which his written utterances were submitted, it is just these written declarations of Constantine that betray that the dogmatic foundations of Christianity remained a mystery to him.[2]

What really gripped this son of an age of decadence, sunk in superstition and mysticism, was not the refined theological system of the Church, not the lofty moral teaching of the New Testament, but its unbounded faith in the limitless power of Christ.[3] From it he expected the prosperity of his Empire in peace and its victory in war. So true is it that power was for him the deciding factor, that he did not attach himself to Christ until Christ had fulfilled His promise to lend him His aid. Here we see a survival of that way of thinking that characterizes ancient paganism: *votum solvit libens merito*—to quote the expression of thousands of dedicatory inscriptions. From the Christian standpoint, no doubt, this meant a serious decline in the standard of belief. Just before the time of Constantine whole generations of confessors had gladly submitted to the bitterest afflictions from the mighty ones of this world of shadows, to win their rich reward in the hereafter. In complete contrast to them, the basis of the religious convictions of Constantine was success on earth. His successes in war and peace were represented by him to the world as the proof of the rightness of his confession. Nor was he alone in this. The learned Church historian Eusebius, the highly

[1] H. Lietzmann, *Gesch. d. alten Kirche*, iii, 1938, 151 and note 4.

[2] Ibid. 113 and 151; id. *Sitzungsbericht. Preuss. Akad.* 1937, 274. Cf. also, for example, L. Salvatorelli, *Ricerche religiose*, iv, 1928, 318 f.; W. Hartmann, 'Konstantin d. Gr. als Christ und Philosoph in seinen Briefen u. Erlassen' (*Beilage z. Progr. d. stadt. Gymn. zu Fürstenwalde*, Ostern, 1902), 16 f., endeavours in vain to supply a philosophical background to Constantine's general phrases.

[3] G. Boissier, op. cit. 35; L. Wrzoł, *Weidenauer Studien*, i, 1906, 266 f.; A. Manaresi, *L'Impero romano e il cristianesimo*, 1914, 511 f.; F. Lot, *La Fin du monde antique*, 1927, 35 f.; H. M. D. Parker, *A History of the Roman World from 138 to 337 A.D.*, 1935, 303; K. Müller, *Kirchengeschichte*, i², 1929, 363; O. Seeck, op. cit. i⁴, 57 f., &c.

educated rhetorician and apologist Lactantius, and others with them, said precisely the same, and not a voice was raised in denial. It is the increasing spread of ideas of primitive religion and magic in that age that explains the exceptional part played in the story of Constantine's conversion by the initial letters of the name of Christ. We see no more in such symbols than purely abstract reminders; but, then, the most palpable magical potency was ascribed to them.[1] Let us listen, for example, to what Lactantius has to say of the amazing efficacy of the sign of the Cross.

'How terrified the demons are by this sign may be realized, if you observe how, when conjured by the name of Christ, they take their flight from the bodies that they have possessed. . . . The case is not hard to prove. . . . When the pagans sacrifice to their gods, the sacred act misses its effect, if a single person is present, whose brow is signed with the Cross. This was often the very reason why wicked rulers persecuted the Christian righteousness. When those tyrants were sacrificing and certain of our community were present in their train, those Christian brethren, by signing their brows with the Cross, put the gods to flight, so that they could not reveal the future from the entrails of the beasts. The 'haruspices', observing this, at the instigation of those very demons, for whom they were performing their dissections, raised the complaint that 'profane' persons were present, disturbing the sacred acts. Thus they moved their princes to fury and drove them to try and storm the Church of God.'[2]

The motives that led Diocletian and Galerius to set on foot the persecution of the Church were of a different order, but there can be no doubt that they, too, were troubled by the fear of magic signs. Their eyes, like those of Constantine, were dazzled by the conceptions of a world of mechanical magic, that to us seem so simple-minded. Everyone was then convinced that you could bring the supernatural powers into your service by magic signs, formulas, and rites. Feverish, then, was the quest for such miraculous forms and devices. The Church itself could not quite escape from this atmosphere of fog. We must not fail to notice that Eusebius, for example, regularly describes the divine sign, which, in his account,

[1] See Note 7, p. 126.   [2] See Note 8, p. 127.

helped Constantine to victory, as a magic charm. Not only
does he place on record all the wonderful tales that Constantine
had told him of the miracles performed by the *labarum*, the
banner with the initial letters of Christ, but he elaborates them
with obvious delight.[1] At a later date Constantine made use
of other talismans of Christian character—such as nails from
the Redeemer's Cross. One such nail he set in his golden
diadem, with its jewelled mount, another in the snaffle of
his war-horse. Bishop Ambrose, one of the most brilliant intel-
lects of the century, speaks of such talismans with veneration
and wonder. . . .[2] It was no mere accident, either, that our
Emperor made trial of the magic power of the Christian monogram just before a battle on the issue of which hung life and
death. Human weakness generally turns to heaven when little
help can be expected on earth. And there was also a special
reason. We have already seen that, since the age of the
Antonines, more trust had been placed in the prayers of the
Emperor, facing such a decision, than on his arms. The spirit
of the age insisted that an Emperor, in such a case, must assure
himself of the help of the heavenly powers.[3] From now on it
was the victory of the ruler that decided the rightness of his
religion: that victory was taken as the arbitrament of the true
God.

The Christianity of Constantine, then, was not wrapped in the
glory of the true Christian spirit, but in the darkness of superstition. But to deny the sincerity and urgency of his religious
convictions is to make a very grave mistake.[4] The vision of
Constantine swept him off his feet, and its effects far outweighed
the bombastic story of wonder in Eusebius.

On the evening of the 27th of October A.D. 312 the monogram, without a spectacular *mise en scène* and with hardly a
sound, entered on its brilliant march of triumph. A considerable part of the army hardly knew, it seems, what the sign,
painted on their shields, meant. Before the decisive battle was
fought, Constantine could not have trumpeted it abroad that

[1] See Note 9, p. 127.
[2] Ambros. *De obitu Theodos.* 47, p. 61, ed. M. D. Mannix.
[3] Cf. my remarks in *Pisciculi*, 17.
[4] So O. Seeck, op. cit. i[4]. 56.

he had placed himself and his soldiers under the protection of Christ. He would have been risking a serious reaction on the part of the pagans. At the entry into Rome the sign, conspicuous on the shields of the men, may have begun to arouse attention, may even, here and there, have provoked resentment, but certainly no serious reaction. Nor can Constantine's first measures in favour of the Christians have occasioned any particular excitement in Rome. There had already been the Edict of Toleration and the similar conduct of Maxentius. Constantine's touch was gentle and he was able to avoid any violent convulsions. There was no radio in those days, no loudspeakers or similar instruments of modern publicity, to broadcast exciting news in the twinkling of an eye. The Donatist bishops, as Fr. Stähelin has rightly emphasized,[1] when they wished to flatter Constantine simply declared that they had confidence in him because of his father, who had held back from the persecutions. Of his own Christian confession of faith they said nothing—probably because they knew nothing. More remarkable still is the circumstance that Lactantius, who certainly knew of the new turn of events when he wrote a little later about the 'Deaths of the Persecutors', does not celebrate Constantine as the one and only champion of the cause of the Church and as the exclusive favourite of the Lord. Licinius shares in the miraculous aid of God.[2] No one, then, had any idea of how far Constantine intended to go in his favours to the Church. But he himself was quite sure.

[1] Optat. Milevit. *De schismate Donat.* 1. 22 (H. v. Soden, *Urkunden*, S. 13): 'Rogamus te Constantine optime imperator, quoniam de genere iusto es, cuius pater inter ceteros persecutores persecutionem non exercuit.' Attention to these important facts is called by F. Staehelin, *Zeitschrift f. Schweizerische Geschichte*, xvii, 1937, 408.

[2] Lactant. *De mort. pers.* 46. 1 ff., especially 2: 'Tunc proxima nocte Licinio quiescenti adsistit angelus dei monens ut ocius surgeret atque oraret deum summum cum omni exercitu suo: illius fore victoriam, si fecisset. . .' Cf. ibid. 44. 5: 'Commonitus est in quiete Constantinus, ut caeleste signum dei notaret in scutis atque ita proelium committeret.' Licinius naturally received high praise in the first edition of the *Church History* of Eusebius, too. Cf. Ed. Schwartz, *RE.* vi. 1403 ff.; Eusebius later suppressed his earlier view. Cf. Joh. Straub, *Vom Herrscherideal der Spätantike*, 1939, 104.

III

THE MOVING FORCES IN THE RELIGIOUS POLICY OF CONSTANTINE AND ITS INITIAL DIFFICULTIES

SEEN through the eyes of Jacob Burckhardt,[1] the revolution begun by Constantine was the work of a cold and calculating politician, who kept his own personal convictions in the background till the last possible moment. The ideas of that great thinker are still working to-day.[2] But O. Seeck, manfully overcoming his antipathy to the Church, has already proved that Constantine's resolve was produced by religious enlightenment and not by political calculation; and Norman Baynes has used Constantine's own expressions in writing to demonstrate the religious motives of his action, while also finally establishing the authenticity of the documents.

The decisions of a ruler take shape in a series of political acts; but the motives and feelings that give them birth are not irrelevant to the question. Constantine himself could not leave out of account the probable effects that his new line of policy might produce. It cannot have escaped his notice that, once the traditional policy of the State in dealing with the Christians had gone bankrupt, the toleration of Galerius and the benevolence of Maxentius only represented partial solutions. An institution as all-embracing and aggressive as the Church, ambitious, too, to win the monopoly in interpreting the sum of things, could not finally be satisfied with them. We must therefore recognize in Constantine's support and

---

[1] J. Burckhardt, *Die Zeit Constantins des Grossen*[5], 334.

[2] The arguments of E. Caspar, *Geschichte des Papsttums*, i, 1930, 107 f., according to which 'Stronger than religious feeling in determining his relation to Christianity was political calculation', are refuted by what K. Müller has to say in his *Kirchengeschichte*, i[2], 1929, 361 f. Farther than anyone else in his denial of the Christian sentiment of Constantine has gone H. Grégoire, the great Belgian Byzantinist, in his *Revue de l'Université de Bruxelles*, xxxvi, 1930, i. 231 ff.; he has been followed by many others. Against the view of Burckhardt, Th. Keim raised his voice long ago in *Der Übertritt Constantins zum Christentum*, 1862, 676.

favouring of the Church the same consistency that the State
had hitherto shown in denying and persecuting it. However
true it may be for Constantine that it was through the channels
of religious feeling that every favour to the Christians found its
way into the stream of politics,[1] we must not overlook the fact
that the measures taken at the same time in this field by his
colleagues in every case subordinated the element of emotion
to political calculation: we mean, for example, the initial
favour shown to the Christians by Licinius, the toleration
granted by Maximin, under pressure from him, and the subsequent change of front by Licinius. But it is just here that
the greatness of Constantine is revealed. However often he
changes his tactics, there are no breaks in his strategy.

After the 28th of October A.D. 312 Constantine could not wipe
out the pagans overnight any more than he could at one stroke
raise Christianity to be the sole religion of the State. The two
irreconcilable powers stood confronted, with equal rights—but
not with equal favour. This gave rise to unpleasantness and
confusion. Modern scholars have seldom been able to understand the Janus face of this short period of transition. Attempts
have been made to get rid of the cleavage by simply denying
that Constantine was a partisan of the Christians or, conversely,
by erasing the obvious traces of his pagan connexions and
obligations. Others, again, have tried to discover, in place of
the real ambiguity implied in the position, a similar ambiguity
in Constantine himself[2] or contradictions in his behaviour.[3]
'A poor fumbler' is Piganiol's description of him,[4] while even

[1] J. Bidez, *L'Antiquité class.* i, 1932, 5, expresses this thought thus: 'In
the mind of a statesman may not mysticism and calculation exist together?
May not the inspirations of the Spirit show themselves in the form of considered reflection? The life of the Emperor, Julian, is full of inspirations of
this kind. Well, in many respects, the clairvoyant of the caves of Mithras
was like enough to his uncle, the devotee of a Gallic sanctuary.' See also, for
example, L. Salvatorelli, *Rivista storica italiana*, N.S. 5, xliv, 1927, 167 f.,
and id., *Ricerche religiose*, iv, 1928, 290.

[2] See Note 10, p. 127.

[3] A. Manaresi, op. cit. 513: 'Why Constantine appears in history as one
continuous contradiction.' L. Bréhier, *Rev. hist.* cxix, 1915, 258: '. . . The
actions of Constantine in his religious policy reveal a certain hesitation, a
slightly equivocal character. . . .'

[4] A. Piganiol, op. cit. 226.

Norman Baynes sees in his religious policy a 'conscious ambiguity'.[1] His actions in these years, it is maintained, do not correspond to the expressions of favour to the Church which he published.[2] Lietzmann has an explanation of this supposed double-dealing:[3] Constantine conducted himself as a Christian before Christians, but not in public, so long as ever he feared that any other course of action might prove politically disadvantageous. To this we can only reply, with Seeck,[4] that it is really too naïve to suppose that Constantine, in an age of such sharply defined contrasts between two religions, could possibly steer his way through without letting the adherents of either realize where his true allegiance belonged. The ordinances of the Emperor were not sent out in secret, and they did not lose their general validity when they happened to be addressed to Christian governors. And how can we reconcile with this supposed 'secret Christian' attitude of Constantine the confession implied in the initials of Christ on his helmet? Their appearance on issues of coins from all quarters, soon after the defeat of Maxentius, loudly and unmistakably proclaimed where Constantine stood. Lietzmann in another passage[5] has clearly realized the contradiction implied in his own assumption. 'There is a line running straight from Constantine's youth to his death, and the same unity may be seen in his religious policy as in his political activity. He was a man of a single mould. He knew from the first what he meant to do, and he had the strength to do it.'

We tend involuntarily to conceive of the conversion of

[1] *C.A.H.* xii, 1939, 685.

[2] H. v. Campenhausen, *Deutsche Literaturzeitung*, 1933, 1212; F. Stähelin, op. cit. 414 f.

[3] H. Lietzmann, *Sitzungsber. d. Preuss. Akad.* 1937, 274.

[4] O. Seeck, op. cit. i[4]. 60 f.: 'For it is naïve, indeed, to suppose that, in an age of such sharply defined religious contrasts, he could tack in and out between the two creeds, without the believers in either knowing to which he really belonged.'

[5] H. Lietzmann, ibid. 275: 'Es ist eine Linie, die von seiner Jugend bis zu seinem Tode gradlinig verläuft und damit auch in der religiösen Haltung Konstantins dieselbe Einheit erkennen lässt, welche seine politische Wirksamkeit charakterisiert. Dieser Mann ist aus einem Guss, wusste von Anfang an, was er wollte, und besass auch die Kraft, es auch zu erreichen.'

Constantine in terms that have actually been true in millions of cases. Driven by the longing for moral regeneration, or whatever may have been the motive for submission, men have humbly knocked at the door of the Church, have received gracious admission, and have proceeded to regulate their lives by the rules of that community—no matter who they be, poor devils or kings. But there is nothing in common between the case of Constantine and these normal phenomena. It is quite another story. The mightiest man on earth inclines to a belief in Christ and, before he finally surrenders, takes warning from a dream and makes trial of the power of Christ's name. When the sacred initials have actually proved their supernatural power and their miraculous efficacy, Constantine adopts the cause of Christianity and gradually pushes it into the foreground of his whole conception of the State.

But still, though he supports and exalts the Church, it is as one who stands above and outside it, of his own free decision, without any attachment to its organization. And thus he still remains the head of the official religion of pagan polytheism. The Church has no right to prescribe to him, can only look up to him with heart-felt gratitude.[1] At last she can draw free breath and rejoices in her new-won freedom ; she does not yet go on to think of the serious destruction of her adversaries. The pagans, for their part, still celebrate the lord of the world as a supernatural being in their traditional forms of cult ; yes, they still honour their lawful lord, even while he is cutting away the ground from under their feet.

This is no case of a revolution led by a group, hitherto without rights and oppressed, hastening to turn the world upside down. The existence of paganism is not threatened by elements breaking through from below—it is the holder of the armed forces who suddenly sets himself to oust it. His first steps are slow and conciliatory, but his purpose is plain and unambiguous.

Constantine did not intend to use force. He must, therefore, use a cautious strategy to shatter the position of paganism—often making a wise retirement after the failure of one attack, but always pushing forward again with redoubled fury. But, all the time, as we shall see, he keeps on shedding those relics

[1] See Note 11, p. 128.

of his old creed, which he could not abandon immediately after the Mulvian Bridge, like the butterfly that still trails its slough behind it as it creeps out of its cocoon, until at last it can be rid of it altogether. As this happened, it was the mixed pagan religions that gradually came to take the place of Christianity as merely tolerated bodies. Plain evidences of intolerance towards them were already to be seen here and there.

All this involves a certain hesitancy. Owing to the scantiness of our sources it cannot always be fully demonstrated, but it can hardly have been different in kind from the conduct of Constantine in the course of the struggle with the Donatists or the dispute with the Arians. Under the influence of a strong personality or the pressure of one of the two opposing parties, Constantine repeatedly shifted his position, but without ever losing sight of his final aim.[1] We shall observe the same pliancy in his dealings with the pagans of Rome. Just as the tacking of a sailing-boat is only designed to make full use of the wind, without giving up direction, so too with Constantine's changes of attitude.

This conclusion is not invalidated by the fact that Constantine's shifts were not always due to cold-blooded calculation. He often fell into a fury, and then his passions knew no control. It was this blind anger that sealed the fate of his rivals and of others who vexed him. The guilt of these political murders may be ascribed, in part, to the cruel spirit of the age; but no such excuse can be found for his murder of his own wife and his own eldest son.[2] The Church of the West was well aware why it could not number Constantine among its saints. Even in religious matters his unbridled anger could lead him to quite unexpected decisions, as is shown in his disputes with the Arians.[3] His dramatic clash with the pagans of Rome sprang from just such an outbreak of passion. And yet, in a

[1] V. Schultze writes very truly, op. cit. 58 f.: 'However little the religious policy of Constantine fails to do justice to the cleverness and cautious reflection of its author and director, it is never one that wanders aimlessly to and fro. On the one hand, it reveals the amazing talent of Constantine for being either merciless or considerate, as circumstances demanded, but it shows, on the other hand, his firm will in its bent towards its goal.'

[2] Cf., for example, L. Wrzoł, *Weidenauer Studien*, i, 1906, 248 ff., &c.

[3] Athanas. *Apol. contra Ar.* 87. 2.

late return to sobriety, he would repeal commands given in wrath. His final aims were never upset by his impetuosity.[1] To understand the religious policy of Constantine it is important to realize that it was dynamic, not static.[2] Roman policy, in applying its traditional measures to ensure the loyalty of its subjects and to prevent forbidden associations, had been inspired by the endeavour to maintain peace and social equilibrium at home. Not so with the policy of Constantine. It was rather like the succession of steps taken by a general who shapes his tactics to suit the expediencies of battle. From the time that Constantine first made use of the magical initial letters in the great battle at the gates of Rome, he kept on intensifying his interventions in the interests of the Church. Both in his ideals and in his practice he moved farther and farther away from paganism until, in a quarter of a century, he had completely revolutionized the relations between the State and the rival religions. We shall follow this process step by step, and we shall see that it was accomplished in three stages. The first lasted until the tension preceding the settlement with Licinius—that is to say, from A.D. 312 to 320. During this period Constantine hardly touches paganism, but exalts the Church with increasing energy. In the second stage he thrusts the organization of the Church into the foreground of public life and, at the same time, directs a frontal attack on polytheism—A.D. 320 to 330. Finally, in the last period, he breaks all but a few of the threads that still bind him to the national past and wages open war on the old religions from his new capital in the East. If death had not stopped him he would of a surety have forbidden them entirely. It was only with the

[1] The character of Constantine was really like the description given by Philostorgios, following an earlier source, which is summed up by our best authority on Philostorgios in the following terms: 'We see him on every occasion just as brutal and decided as he is farsighted and intelligent. Too practical and hurried to have any scruples in his choice of ways and means, he loves to show himself, now loyal, sweet and charming, but, again, on occasion, he cheats, he pretends, then, all of a sudden, strikes and savages. Above all, he is a man of action.' J. Bidez, *Byzantion*, x, 1935, 412 f.

[2] As recently supposed by J. R. Knipfing, *Catholic Historical Review*, N.S. iv, 1924, 501, or R. Laqueur, *Probleme der Spätantike*, 1930, 8 f. For a similar view, cf. J. Geffcken, *Der Ausgang des griech.-röm. Heidentums*, 1920, 96 f.

religious traditions of the city of Rome that he did not yet
venture to meddle. This threefold division in the religious policy of Constantine
was recognized by the pagans themselves. As it implied for
them a progressive oppression and ruin, their historians have
made use of the scheme of the advancing degeneration of the
tyrant to describe the reign of Constantine.[1] It is an elaborate
device, familiar from the beginnings of Greek literature to the
end of the Roman period, for venting hostility on a person in
authority.[2]

Let us now cast a hasty glance at the forces that drove Constantine on the path that we have been indicating. First
among these forces was his own revolutionary character, described by Julian in the words, 'novator turbatorque prisca-
rum legum et moris antiquitus recepti', 'a wicked innovator
and tamperer with the time-hallowed laws and the sacred
ethical traditions of our fathers'.[3] Constantine's passion for
change[4] found boundless opportunity for exercise in his omnipotence as Emperor. In every field of public life his reforms
aimed at unification, and in this reduction of all affairs of life
to the common denominator of the absolute Empire the
promotion of uniformity in the Church had its part. At this
point his endeavours met and harmonized with the aims of the
Church.[5]

But the religious policy of Constantine derived its driving
force, not only from his natural capacities, but also from his
Christian conviction—and this was far from being as mild and
gentle as, in the spirit of the Gospels, it should have been.

[1] Eutrop. x. 6. 3: 'Verum insolentia rerum secundarum aliquantum Constantinus ex illa favorabili animi docilitate mutavit.'
[2] Basing himself on the three periods—*praestantissimus, latro, pupillus*—in
the *Epitome de Caesaribus*, 41, A. Piganiol divided his important book on
Constantine into three sections. But see my comments on the progressive
debasement in the career of the tyrant in classical literature in my paper,
'A gót mozgalom és Dácia pusztulása', offprint from *Archivum Philologicum*,
1929–30, 21 ff.
[3] Ammian. 21. 10. 8.
[4] Eutrop. x. 8. 1: 'Multas leges rogavit, quasdam ex bono et aequo, pleras-
que superfluas, nonnullas severas. . . .'
[5] Ed. Schwartz, *Gött. gel. Nachr.* 1904, 536. Cf. also Th. Keim, op. cit. 50.

Baynes is quite right.[1] This man, with his sudden gusts of passion, certainly conceived of the Almighty as being as quick to wrath as he himself was. Not long after his conversion he writes to an African governor that God bitterly punishes those who shame His honour, whilst He loads with blessings those who serve Him.[2] This is the same atmosphere as that which pervades the pamphlet of Lactantius on the 'Deaths of the Persecutors', which appeared about the same time. It is no mere edifying phrase when Constantine, as early as A.D. 313, tells the Donatists that he expects the judgement of his deeds from Christ.[3]

Beside his fear of God, a true consciousness of mission[4] burned in him. The conception of the ruler, elected and protected by the gods, was common property of the whole of the ancient world. The Great Kings of the Middle East proclaimed their divine mission. From them and from the Pharaohs the awe-inspiring influence of this idea was inherited by the Hellenistic monarchs and the Roman Emperors. Constantine did not, like his predecessors, simply take over his protecting deity—he chose him for himself; and his choice was sealed by a fiery vision that, at the same time, as we have seen, was the call to him to become a prophet. But this prophet did not appear in rags, like others of whom God has taken possession, but in the gold-embroidered, bejewelled robes of the mightiest on earth, lord, not of demon phantoms, but holder, under Heaven, of supreme earthly power, not aiming at enforcing moral regeneration, but promising worldly happiness to all who followed him. This materialization of the spiritual function of prophecy makes a very strange impression on us. But it is the same change that led from the suffering Christianity of earlier generations, with its dream of bliss in the Hereafter, to the Church of the earthly Canaan, the Promised Land, that Constantine opened to the confessors of the new faith.

The proselytizing fervour of Constantine was combined with the iron will that had led him over the corpses of his colleagues to sole rule. In the service of faith it was an irresistible force.

[1] N. H. Baynes, op. cit. 14.   [2] Euseb. *H.E.* x. 7.
[3] Quoted on p. 39, n. 4.
[4] Excellently characterized by Baynes, op. cit. 29.

As early as A.D. 314, in his address to the Synod of Arles,[1] he called himself the *famulus Dei*—a phrase constantly on his lips later.[2] When at last he held the whole Roman Empire under his sole sway, he describes his own activities in the following words:[3]

'When godlessness, far and wide, lay heavy on men, when the State was threatened by the deadly pestilence of utter corruption and a radical cure was the urgent need, what a relief, what a salvation from the mischief did God contrive! . . . God decreed my service and accounted me fit to execute His decree. And thus have I, setting out from the sea in Britain and the lands where the sun must set, driven out and scattered the terrors that ruled on every hand, by power from on High, that mankind, instructed by my mission, might return to the service of the Holy Law and that our most blessed faith might also be spread abroad, under the mighty direction of the Highest. Being convinced that this was my glorious task, this God's gracious gift to me, I come now also to the lands of the East, which, in their bitter pains, require my earnest aid.'

To complete the picture of the work of the imperial missionary we must add the colossal propaganda that he developed in word and picture. The initials of the name of Christ were driven into the general consciousness, as the symbol of the revelation vouchsafed to Constantine by God and of the divine help that came to him in reward for his conversion. In the story, as the Emperor himself told it, the working up of the legend is palpable[4] and this legend was adorned by him with all the hues of fancy, to win adherents for the Holy Faith. Constantine did not wait for the Church to put a halo round his head. The emphasis on the 'I' in the utterances of the missionary of God had long been proper to the proclamations of the Redeemer-Emperor, even in his most commonplace ordinances. But, hitherto, the Emperor had postured as the mythical restorer of the Golden Age, while Constantine must

---

[1] *Appendix Optati Milev.*, no. V = H. v. Soden, 'Urkunden zur Gesch. d. Donatismus', *Kleine Texte*, cxii, 1913, p. 23.

[2] Joh. Straub, op. cit. 246, n. 226, has recently collected a series of passages from the documents in Eusebius.

[3] Euseb. *Vita Const.* 2. 28 and 29.

[4] H. Lietzmann, *Gesch. d. alten Kirche*, iii, 1938, 62.

now find a more modest expression of his role in a Christian
sense.[1]
Apart from the monogram of salvation, the statues, paintings, and coin-types displayed, throughout the Empire, the
gaze of the 'most religious Majesty', directed heavenwards.[2]
Inscriptions on the bases of his statues,[3] on the entrance to his
palace[4] and in other places, proclaimed that Christ had helped
him to vanquish his enemies and win the Empire of the world.
Paintings showed him piercing the snaky dragon of paganism.[5]
The propaganda of the Court was re-echoed by the leading
personalities of the Church, who call Constantine the apostle
of God[6] and extol him as a new Moses.[7] Once, in defining his
own circle of duty, as opposed to that of the bishops, he formu-
lated it thus: they had the charge of human souls inside the
Church, he was ordained by God to perform the same function
for those that were outside it.[8] What he meant by 'those
outside'—whether the pagans, the heretics, or mankind
beyond the frontiers—does not so much matter; what *is* vital
is that he 'certainly meant it to be understood, that he felt the
call to secure consideration for the Church in the eyes of the
whole world and that he intended to validate the decisions of
the Church leaders'.[9] But the form of expression is cautious

---

[1] This is not just an expression of the personal vanity or inflated self-
esteem of Constantine, as, for example, L. Wrzoł supposes, *Weidenauer
Studien*, i, 1906, 251: 'His vanity is certainly shown when he takes such
delight in thinking himself the chosen servant of God, called to conquer His
enemies and evangelize the world.'
[2] H. Lietzmann, op. cit., is wrong in thinking that one could not tell
whether this was actually Christian. See also O. Seeck, *Zeitschr. für Numismatik*, xxi, 1898, 29 f., and my own arguments in '25 Jahre Römisch-Germanische Kommission, 1929', 42 ff.
[3] On the statue in Rome see below.
[4] Mamboury–Th. Wiegand, *Die Kaiserpaläste von Konstantinopel*, 1934, 7 f.
[5] Cf. below, p. 84 f.
[6] Wrongly doubted by Joh. Straub, op. cit., p. 244, no. 211.
[7] E. Becker, *Zeitschrift für Kirchengesch.* xxxi, 1910, 161 ff.
[8] Euseb. *Vita Const.* 4. 24: ἀλλ' ὑμεῖς μὲν τῶν εἴσω τῆς ἐκκλησίας, ἐγὼ δὲ τῶν
ἐκτὸς ὑπὸ θεοῦ καθεσταμένος ἐπίσκοπος ἂν εἴην. Cf. E.-Ch. Babut, *Revue critique
d'histoire et de la litt.* N.S. lxviii, 1909, 362 ff.; E. Caspar, op. cit. i. 117; Joh.
Straub, op. cit. 244 ff., Anm. 218, &c.
[9] G. Boissier, op. cit. i⁸. 58.

and, in my belief, we see here the same caution that made Constantine pay such heed to maintaining the normal forms of discussion in the synods, even when he himself was present, have all decisions taken by the bishops, and only appear himself as the executor of their conclusions. Actually, of course, the bishops were only helping to realize Constantine's own efforts towards the complete unification of the Church. He certainly felt himself to be the bishop of all mankind, a God-appointed Pope, and Eusebius, when he once gave him that name, was hitting the right nail on the head.[1] His secret aspirations carried him into an even higher sphere: he felt that he stood on the same rank as the Apostles of the Lord. Others, it is true, do not go beyond calling him the 'peer of the Apostles'.[2] But, at his own express wish, he was buried in his new capital as the thirteenth Apostle, with the cenotaphs of the disciples of Christ, six and six, to right and left of his grave.[3]

[1] Euseb. *Vita Const.* 1. 44: οἷά τις κοινὸς ἐπίσκοπος ἐκ θεοῦ καθεσταμένος. Cf. ibid. 4. 8: οἷά τις κοινὸς τῶν ἀπανταχοῦ κηδεμών. See also Th. Keim, *Der Übertritt Constantins d. Gr. zum Christentum*, 1862, 49.

[2] For example, following others, Zonaras, xiii. 4. 20 (3, p. 23. 7 Büttner–Wobst) ὁ δ' ἰσαπόστολος αὐτοκράτωρ.

[3] Euseb. *Vita Const.* 4. 60; A. Kaniuth, *Die Beisetzung Konstantins des Grossen*, 1941, 18, 26, 36 ff., 60 ff.; cf. also, A. Heisenberg, *Grabeskirche und Apostelkirche*, 1908, 115 f.; R. Baumstark, *Röm. Quartalschr.*, Suppl. xix, 1912, 253; P. Franchi de' Cavalieri, *Mélanges d'arch. et d'hist.* xxxvi, 1916/17, 240 ff.; H. Koethe, *Jahrbuch d. deutschen Arch. Inst.* xlviii, 1933, 187; O. Weinreich, *Triskaidekadische Studien*, 1916, 12.

IV

THE FIRST PERIOD OF CONSTANTINE'S INDEPENDENT RELIGIOUS POLICY: FROM THE BATTLE OF THE MULVIAN BRIDGE TO THE SECOND PERIOD OF TENSION WITH LICINIUS

(a) *The attitude of Constantine to Christianity*

JULIUS CAESAR, in his day, had had the conviction that only the monarchy could avail to control the vastly increased Empire. He had tried to accomplish at one stroke the fundamental reform of the machinery of the Republic, with all that that implied—a reform that was only completed in fact some two hundred years later. But it was all in vain that Caesar, with his iron logic, realized the principles and consequences of that great change. He under-estimated the forces from which the old constitution drew its strength, and those forces swept him away. It was reserved for his conciliatory successor to fit the pillars of the monarchy—almost surreptitiously—into the structure of the Republic. Now the procedure was reversed. The attempt of the conservative Diocletian to establish the imperial autocracy on the basis of the old Roman ethics and religion failed. The time had now come for that ruthless consistency at which Caesar had aimed in vain. All that was left of the old structure could no longer sustain the rise of the new. It was only the accomplished fact that roused the aristocracy of Rome from its slumbers.

Before Constantine crossed the Tiber it was only with Christ, who held him captive, that he had to reckon. But after his way into Rome had been opened up, he had to do something for the flock of Christ. Its persecution had only just been abandoned by the holders of power and it was still not regarded by the ruling circles as a desirable social organization. The successors of Constantine, no less than his predecessors, were irresistibly carried away by the dazzling past of Rome when once they set foot on her hallowed ground. But on Constantine himself the majestic buildings of the Capitol and the wonderful temples of the old gods had little effect. Revolutionary plans were already fermenting in his brain, and he set to work at once to carry them out.

Constantine did not spend much more than two months in Rome, but he had time to commence his dispositions in favour of the Christians.[1] He was bound to begin by proclaiming legal toleration, based on measures already dictated by the actual position. As the acts of Maxentius had lost their validity he presumably called back into force the Edict of Galerius.[2] There is nothing surprising in this—only that he was not content to assure the freedom of the Christians living in his own domains, but, as early as A.D. 312, brought pressure to bear on Maximin Daza to make him suspend the persecution in the East. Such zeal betrays the fact that he was already converted.[3] Much more important are the efforts that he made to secure the adherence of Licinius to his pro-Christian policy— efforts ending in success, even if only for a time, early in A.D. 313.[4] Even before his agreement with Licinius, Constantine had very probably issued those decrees which Licinius, after him, adopted in Milan,[5] and which we know in the version in which Licinius, after driving out Daza, proclaimed them in the East.[6]

[1] See Note 12, p. 129.

[2] So, recently, J. R. Palanque, following E. Caspar and E. Stein, op. cit. 609. All that we know of the issue of this ordinance is that it was soon withdrawn on the ground of the agreements of Milan, as it was already not liberal enough by then.

[3] Lactant. *De mort. pers.* 36. 3 and 37. 1; Euseb. *H.E.* ix. 9. 12 ff. A. Piganiol, *L'Empereur Constantin*, 1932, 88 ff., rightly sees that 'it is this haste which justifies us in speaking of the miracle of the Mulvian Bridge and of a sudden revelation'; Ed. Schwartz, *Gött. gel. Nachr.* 1904, 528, note 2; O. Seeck, op. cit. i⁴. 147 and 503; N. H. Baynes, *Class. Quarterly*, xviii, 1924, 194; K. Bihlmeyer, *Theol. Quartalschrift*, xciv, 1912, 411 ff., 527 ff., &c.

[4] Cf., for example, P. Batiffol, *La Paix Constantinienne*³, 1914, 260 ff., &c.

[5] We follow here N. H. Baynes, *C.A.H.* xii, 1939, 686: 'Technically it may be true that there was no Edict of Milan, but . . . that is because Constantine had already accorded to all his subjects those rights which were granted to the provinces of Asia in the letter issued at Nicomedia by Licinius a few months later, which itself summarized Constantine's legislation promulgated by him as senior Augustus after the crowning mercy of the Battle of the Mulvian Bridge.'

[6] See Note 13, p. 129.

These measures represent a great step in advance. The
Edict of Galerius had done no more than guarantee the toleration of the Christians; Constantine's will now gave them
equality in law and State.[1] Galerius had only given up the
attempt to suppress the Church; Constantine handsomely in-
demnified it for the property that it had lost.[2] Even if Constantine, in so doing, started out with the idea of the equality
of Christians and pagans, there is more to it than that. The
edict, issued by Licinius, shows that the Emperors owed their
successes to the God of the Christians[3]—or, in other words,
that the Government depended for support upon their God.[4]
In the months that followed the battle at the gates of Rome
we observe that Constantine is already using terms of the
greatest respect for that Christianity for which earlier
Emperors had had only terms of reproach. He describes it as
the 'most holy worship'.[5] It is quite amazing to see with what
hesitation and reticence this man of firm resolve handles the
awkward turn taken by the case of the Donatist sectaries. He
is afraid of God. In a surviving letter, addressed at the end of
A.D. 312 to an African governor, he expresses the conviction
that he owes the triumph over Maxentius to the Christian God,
and he emphasizes the same point a year later in his letter to
the Synod of Arles.[6] He prevailed on Licinius to join him in
public acknowledgement of the same divine assistance.[7] This

---

[1] C. Carassai, *Archivio della R. Società romana di storia patria*, xxiv,
1901, 101.

[2] Lactant. *De mort. pers.* 48. 7–9; Euseb. *H.E.* x. 5. 9 ff.; Ed. Schwartz,
Gött. gel. Nachr. 1904, 535; P. Batiffol, *La Paix Const.*[3], 1914, 249 f.; A.
Piganiol, op. cit. 91 f., &c.

[3] Lactant. *De mort. pers.* 48, 11 and Euseb. *H.E.* ix. 9. 12.

[4] I have already emphasized this in *Pisciculi*, 14; but see also Th. Keim,
Der Übertritt Constantins d. Gr. zum Christentum, 1862, 27, 29.

[5] Euseb. *H.E.* x. 6. 1; cf. x. 5. 20. Similar expressions are collected in
I. Heikel, *Eusebius Werke*, Bd. i, Einleitung, S. lxxxiii, lxxxvi f., lxxxviii;
H. Lietzmann, *Sitzungsberichte d. Preuss. Akad., phil.-hist. Kl.*, 1937, 269.

[6] Euseb. *H.E.* x. 5, 15 ff. (see Baynes, Raleigh Lecture (1930), 69). *Appendix
Optati Milevitani*, no. V, ed. Ziwsa = H. v. Soden, 'Urkunden zur Entste-
hungsgeschichte des Donatismus', *Kleine Texte*, cxxii, 1913, 23. Cf. Ed.
Schwartz, *Kaiser Konstantin und die christliche Kirche*[2], 1936, 62 f., &c.

[7] Lactant. *De mort. pers.* 48. 11: 'Hactenus fiet, ut sicut superius compre-
hensum est, divinus iuxta nos favor, quem in tantis sumus rebus experti,

confession was bound to be brought to general knowledge by the edicts posted up in the market-places,[1] and we shall see later that Constantine, again, on his statues and inscriptions, praises the blessings that Christ had conferred on him. It is no surprise, then, that, in his addresses to Ablabius[2] and to the Synod of Arles,[3] he describes himself as belonging to the Christian church. In the latter document we read that he expects from Christ the judgement on his deeds.[4]

The spectacle of the Christian monogram on works of art and coin-types, the blaze of the initials of Christ on the *labarum*, the new imperial banner, were all propaganda in the modern sense. They make us realize clearly that it was not only to the Christians that Constantine proclaimed his adherence to the Church. Eusebius knows that Constantine not only bore the Christian emblem on his helmet in the fight against Maxentius,[5] but continued to wear it in his golden, bejewelled helmet of state.[6] When, as we have already shown, the representation of this helmet, that was new also in its pattern, soon

per omne tempus prospere successibus nostris cum beatitudine publica perseveret' = Euseb. *H.E.* x. 5. 13: τούτῳ γὰρ τῷ λογισμῷ, καθὼς καὶ προείρηται, ἡ θεία σπουδὴ περὶ ἡμᾶς, ἧς ἐν πολλοῖς ἤδη πράγμασιν ἀπεπειράθημεν, διὰ παντὸς τοῦ χρόνου βεβαίως διαμείναι.

[1] Lactantius, op. cit. 48. 1, refers to the copy that was posted up in Nicomedia. As it was expressly ordered, op. cit. 48. 12, that 'haec scripta et ubique proponere et ad omnium scientiam te perferre conveniet, ut huius benivolentiae nostrae sanctio latere non possit', it is quite inconceivable, though H. Lietzmann and other scholars have suggested it, that Constantine only confessed before Christians 'in secret' that he felt as a Christian.

[2] *Appendix Optati*, no. III, ed. Ziwsa = H. v. Soden, 'Urkunden', S. 18: 'Nam cum apud me certum sit te quoque dei summi esse cultorem confiteor gravitati tuae, quod nequaquam fas esse ducam, ut eiusmodi contentiones et altercationes dissimulentur a nobis, ex quibus forsitan commoveri possit summa divinitas non solum contra humanum genus sed etiam in me ipsum, cuius curae nutu suo caelesti terrena omnia moderanda commisit. . . .' The genuineness of this letter was proved against O. Seeck by Mgr. L. Duchesne, *Mélanges d'histoire et d'archéologie*, x, 1889, 589 ff. For a discussion of the modern literature, see N. H. Baynes, op. cit. 75 ff.

[3] See also V. Schultze, *Zeitschrift f. Kirchengeschichte*, viii, 1886, 520 f.; N. H. Baynes, op. cit. 13 and 78 f.

[4] *Append. Optati*, no. V, ed. Ziwsa = H. v. Soden, 'Urkunden', S. 24: 'meum iudicium postulant [sc. Donatistae], qui ipse iudicium Christi exspecto.'

[5] Euseb. *Vita Const.* I. 31. 4.   [6] *Pisciculi*, 4.

appears on the coins, we cannot possibly regard it as a mere sign of zeal on the part of Christian subordinates. The tiniest detail of the imperial dress was the subject of a symbolism that defined rank, that was hallowed by tradition and regulated by precise rules. Anybody who irresponsibly tampered with it would have incurred the severest penalties. Especially would this have been the case if anyone, without imperial authority, had provided the head-gear of the Emperor with a sign of such serious political importance as that attached to the monogram of Christ. Or can one imagine, for example, that the cap of the King of England could be adorned by a chamberlain or court-painter with a swastika or sickle and hammer—without the consent of the King?

I have tried in another place to show how the monogram was first used for propaganda inside a small issue of coins, of late A.D. 312 or early 313, from Treves, the capital of western Europe. It diverges so far from the commonplace types of the period that it can only have been produced at the instance of the highest authority.[1] The issue is of three types: the coins of denarius size were issued in mass; of the series of large medallions of the same types we have only feeble traces left.[2] The obverse and reverse of one coin represent Licinius as Jupiter, those of a second show Maximin Daza as Sol; the third belongs to Constantine, but he is represented simply as a human being, as Emperor in armour on the obverse, while the two Victories of the reverse simply announce victory and promise happiness, and were retained in this sense by Constantine's successors. Otto Voetter, the first to recognize the composition of this special issue, was inclined to assume an identification of Constantine with Mars—to balance his two god-colleagues. But he forgot that the punctilio for precedence in that age would never have allowed that the Emperor who stood first in rank should be represented by a god who stood third. And, moreover, whereas Mars naturally appears with his old, time-honoured attributes, particularly the old-style helmet that he

[1] I have discussed this at length in *J.R.S.* xxii, 1932, 12 ff. and pl. IV. 11–13; also in *Pisciculi*, 3.

[2] Only the type of Constantine is yet known, and in bronze: published by me in *Acta Archaeologica*, v, 1934, 100.

wears on his famous statues, the bust of Constantine in the issue of Treves has a helmet of modern shape[1] which proves beyond doubt that its wearer was a mortal, not a god. So, too, the short sword, with eagle-tip, was a regular emblem of the Emperor,[2] never the attribute of a god.

This must mean, at the least, that the first Augustus, in his own domain, declined to be identified with Jupiter or Sol and chose to appear as a mere man by the side of his god-colleagues. Why did he so choose? Was he not at that very moment concerned with another divine protector? Is it not most remarkable, under these circumstances, that this very coin-type of Constantine, with its new and characteristic shape of helmet and the *Victoriae laetae principis perpetui* on the reverse, was revived some years later in most of the mints of Constantine, and that in the mint of Siscia the monogram of Christ appeared on the helmet instead of a star? It is interesting to notice that on the first coins of Siscia the monogram is represented with exact precision, but is gradually reduced to a mere star—that is to say, that the pattern sent out by the imperial chancellery showed the magic sign clearly, but that in the hands of the local die-sinkers it degenerated into a conventional symbol of star shape, as indeed it appears in other mints.[3] On this combined evidence, I think, we may regard it as certain that the little stars on the helmet of Constantine in the Treves issue of A.D. 312 to 313 were themselves the careless copies of the monogram of Christ. The coin-types of this period are, in every case, mere feeble copies of those great works of art that have not come down to us;[4] and, in this case, too, we must believe that the model of the Treves issue was a group of statuary or a painting in which, beside the two god-kings, stood the protégé of the Christian God.

---

[1] *Acta Archaeologica*, v, 1934, 99 ff.   [2] *Römische Mitteilungen*, l, 1935, 66 f.

[3] Cf. my observations in *Rivista Italiana di Numismatica*, 1921, 7 ff., 45 ff.; *J.R.S.* xxii, 1932, 11 f.

[4] As, for example, on the common coin-types of Diocletian and Herculius as senior Augusti, with the legend, *providentia deorum quies Augg.*, cf. Lactantius' words in *De mort. pers.* 42. 1, 'et quia senes ambo simul plerumque picti erant, et imagines simul deponebantur amborum', &c. One sees how what appears on the coins in shortened form and reduced scale was at the same time represented throughout the Empire in greater detail on large canvases.

Eusebius expressly states that Constantine enlisted the plastic art in his campaign to convert the world;[1] and, as luck will have it, we have unimpeachable accounts of a most remarkable example of such propaganda on the part of the imperial missionary, immediately after his entry into Rome. Eusebius,[2] writing in A.D. 314, mentions that the statue of Constantine in Rome itself announced the aid that Christ had given him in his victory, and, a little later, he gives us detailed information about it.[3] The statue in Rome, which he describes, represented the Emperor with standard in hand, on which blazed the monogram of Christ in gold and precious stones.[4] The inscription on the base asseverated that Constantine by this miraculous and blessed sign, τούτῳ τῷ σωτηριώδει σημείῳ, had freed the Eternal City from the yoke of tyranny. This statue represented a new artistic type, in this very point, that, till then, the imperial standard had always been shown in the hand of a standard-bearer of the guard. That the Emperor should take the ensign into his own supreme hand emphasizes its enhanced importance for the future. This new type of statue, in the sequel, gained extraordinary popularity; so we must infer from its uncommon frequency on the coins. Most significant, perhaps, of all is the bronze issue of A.D. 350 with the words *hoc signo victor eris* round the statue of Constantine.[5]

For Constantine, then, after the Mulvian Bridge, the monogram of Christ on his general's standard and his imperial helmet meant two distinct things at once—a talisman to avert harm and bring victory in all his future conflicts, and a con-

---

[1] Euseb. *Vita Const.* 3. 3 and 49; 4. 15, 21, cf. 69.

[2] Euseb. *H.E.* x. 4. 16.

[3] Ibid. ix. 9, 10–11; repeated in *Vita Const.* 1. 40; cf. N. H. Baynes, *Class. Quarterly*, xviii, 1924, 193 f.

[4] And not with the sign of the Cross; see my remarks in *Pisciculi*, 7 ff. In the same place I have tried to show how the Church later endeavoured to replace the monogram of the Redeemer by the sign of the Cross, which corresponded better to its own traditions. See also V. Schultze, *Zeitschr. f. Kirchengeschichte*, vii, 1885, 343 ff., and xiv, 1893, 510 ff. Other views, which I have refuted, will be found in H. Grégoire, *L'Antiquité classique*, i, 1935, 135 ff.; N. H. Baynes, Raleigh Lecture (1930), 60 ff.; J. Gagé, *Revue d'histoire et de philosophie religieuses*, 1933, 385 ff.; H. Lietzmann, *Geschichte d. alten Kirche*, iii, 141, &c.

[5] Cf. *Pisciculi*, 10 f.

fession that he took the side of Christianity. This is just what he emphasizes in his letter to the African proconsul, Anullinus.[1] Not only does he owe his own good fortune in war to the God in whom the Christians trust, but the grace of that same God will bring great blessings on the Empire, whereas neglect of His honour would involve serious afflictions. In an edict of A.D. 314[2] we already find explicit the conception of the Head of the State ruling by the Grace of the Christian God. He writes: 'I, to whose guardianship God has committed the administration of all earthly affairs by His heavenly will.'[3] If any reader is still inclined to minimize the actual significance of this new Christian claim to world-rule, on the plea that Constantine only ventured to use such expressions 'inside', to his fellow believers, he should cast a glance at the festival coins in silver struck in A.D. 315 at Ticinum. Not only does Constantine bear the monogram of Christ on his imperial helmet, but, instead of the sceptre, he bears on his shoulder the Cross of Christ with the globe on top,[4] again announcing, in the language of art, to the whole community of the Roman Empire his call to rule the world in the name of Christ.

The same complex of thought, which had now become the driving motive of Constantine's actions, may be recognized again in a little pamphlet of the period—now set in a larger context and developed in full. The hero of this extraordinary document is the elect favourite of God—Constantine, whose bright figure is set off with great effect against the dark lurking shapes of the past, the persecutors, worse than the Devil himself. I mean, of course, the little book of Lactantius on the 'Deaths of the Persecutors',[5] as horrible and exciting as a

---

[1] Euseb. *H.E.* x. 7. Other passages above, p. 38, n. 6.

[2] *Appendix Optati*, no. III, Ziwsa = H. v. Soden, 'Urkunden', S. 18.

[3] 'Me ipsum, cuius curae nutu suo caelesti terrena omnia moderanda commisit.' On the authenticity of this passage, cf. as against O. Seeck, the arguments of L. Duchesne, *Mélanges d'archéologie et d'histoire*, x, 1890, 589 ff.; N. H. Baynes, Raleigh Lecture (1930), 75 ff.   [4] See Note 14, p. 129.

[5] *Pisciculi*, 6, note 21 (Literatur); see also O. Seeck, *Geschichte d. Unterg. d. ant. Welt*, i[4], 460; Borleffs, *Mnemosyne*, lviii, 1930, 223. The striking agreement of Lactantius' world of thought with that of Constantine can also be demonstrated from Constantine's legislation; see J. Vogt, *Festschr. f. L. Wenger*, ii, 1944, 118 ff.

criminal romance. Written with lively imagination, under the
immediate impression of revolting horrors, it is spiced with
expressions that come straight from the common folk and
flows in easy style. The fresh, quick pulse of its action, the
dialogues, so dramatically introduced, the evil characters of
the Emperors who are being defamed, printed in glowing
colours, the hair-raising tales of terror, must have kept the
contemporary reader in a fever of excitement from beginning
to end. 'Lo, all enemies are blotted out, peace is everywhere
restored', he writes in his introduction, 'and the Church, so
recently beaten low, raises herself again and the temple of God,
which the godless had destroyed, is rebuilt by the mercy of our
God with increased glory. For God has created good rulers,
who have annihilated the lawless and bloody despotism of
tyrants and have given heed to the welfare of mankind; and
already the cheerful light of gentle, lovely peace irradiates the
spirit of man, now that the clouds of those woeful days are
scattered. Those who had the effrontery to wrestle with God
lie vanquished. Those who destroyed the holy temple crash in
heavier ruin themselves.'[1]

The ordinance of Licinius was based on agreements reached
with Constantine at Milan; it was at Nicomedia in June 313
that Lactantius read it.[2] Constantine, who was then in the
West, cannot therefore have borrowed such of his thoughts as
correspond so closely to the 'Deaths of the Persecutors' from
him. The relation of the rulers of the State to God is expressed
in much the same way by both, but, clearly, it is a general idea
of the time. Constantine's attitude becomes the more intelligible, his action the more to be expected, if the circles in
which it could find an echo were so wide. But we must look
at the question from the other side. Was not the Christian

[1] Lactant. *De mort. pers.* 1. 2 ff.: 'Ecce deletis omnibus adversariis, restituta per orbem tranquillitate, profligata nuper ecclesia rursus exsurgit et
maiore gloria templum dei, quod ab impiis fuerat eversum, misericordia
domini fabricatur. Excitavit enim deus principes qui tyrannorum nefaria et
cruenta imperia resciderunt, humano generi providerunt, et iam quasi
discusso tristissimi temporis nubilo mentes omnium pax iucunda et serena
laetificat ... Qui illuctati erant deo, iacent, qui templum sanctum everterant,
ruina maiore ceciderunt.'
[2] Ibid. 48. 1.

rhetorician, with his booklet that aimed at stirring up and inflaming the masses, enrolled in the service of Constantine? The original aim, certainly, was different; for it was in the East, in joyful enthusiasm at the end of the persecutions, that Lactantius penned his aggressive book. He seems to have finished it before the end of A.D. 313.[1] But all indications suggest[2] that the last two chapters were added subsequently, some year and a half later.[3] This appendix, in fact, shows a change of attitude towards Licinius. He is certainly displayed at the outset as a creature of the hated Galerius—even though not reviled as such[4]—and, even later, he is treated with a certain coolness;[5] but, towards the end, he is celebrated with the same enthusiasm as Constantine, as a partaker in the wonderful help of God. But, in the last section,[6] the brutality of Licinius is brought out and the sympathy of the author for the imperial ladies, executed by him, is clearly expressed.[7] All these changes of tempo reflect the political vicissitudes of those years, and the revulsion from Licinius at the close must be connected with the tension between Licinius and Constantine which led to war in A.D. 314, and with the fact that Lactantius then ranged himself on the side of Constantine. This decided championship of the Western Emperor, who favoured the Christians, together with the abrupt rejection of his rival, whom he had only just before been lauding as the elect ruler,

[1] See K. Roller, *Die Kaisergeschichte in Laktanz de mortibus persecutorum*, Diss., 1927, 20 f. It is correct that the description of the death of Diocletian, c. 42. 2–4, does not affect the date, for this account hangs closely together with the description of the overthrow of the common statues of Diocletian and Herculius, and cannot, therefore, be far separated from it in time, whether it is fact or not. Lactantius' pamphlet is dated by J. Vogt, *Zeitschr. f. Kirchengeschichte*, 1942, 187, following Borleffs, to A.D. 318.

[2] So Roller, op. cit.; but he would also assume that Lactantius, with his writing in the East, meant to warn Licinius against a policy of hostility to Christianity. I cannot believe this.

[3] The murder of Valeria fifteen months after the victory of Licinius over Daza gives the *terminus post quem*, op. cit. 51.

[4] Op. cit. 20. 3–4.

[5] Op. cit. 36.

[6] Op. cit. 45. 1 ff., especially 45. 8–48. 13. The 'principes' of the introduction refer to this.

[7] Op. cit. 50. 2 ff.

allows us to infer that Lactantius had, somehow or other, formed a relationship with Constantine. Perhaps it was on the strength of the aggressive pamphlet that Constantine brought the Christian author to his court to be tutor to his eldest son.[1] The final chapter, by its hostility to Licinius, shows that, when it was added, Lactantius was no longer within reach of the Eastern Emperor. The publication, in this final form, seems therefore to have followed in the West under the protection of Constantine. The moral support of the literary propagandist must have confirmed the Emperor's steps on the new path that he had entered. Let us study those steps a little farther.

Constantine, after entering Rome, set to work, not only to build up full legal equality for a Christianity still helpless after the sufferings of the long campaign of persecution, but also to forward and foster the Church politically.[2] Here we see an initiative, as entirely novel as it was bold, which led to an entirely new development. Our information on the matter deals with North Africa. When Constantine had succeeded in adding the North African provinces to his domains, he not only ordered the complete restoration of all Church property,[3] but also arranged for the payment of contributions, no doubt involving large sums of money,[4] to the Catholic communities of those provinces through the organs of his financial administration. Quite apart from this material assistance that was required by the exigencies of the occasion, he thereby laid the foundation of the rise of a vast Church fortune, as also by entitling later on the Christian communities to receive legacies.[5]

[1] Those who have refused to accept the conversion of Constantine in A.D. 312 have naturally refused also to believe that Crispus can have had a Christian tutor before A.D. 317. After what we have said there can be no doubt that this might have been true any time after 28 October A.D. 312. J. Vogt also emphasizes that Crispus need not have been Caesar when Lactantius was attached to him.

[2] For the literature and chronology of the sources, see N. H. Baynes, Raleigh Lecture (1930), 68 f.

[3] Euseb. *H.E.* x. 5. 15 ff.

[4] Ibid. x. 6. 1 ff. Cf. Baynes, op. cit. 16. Probably these ordinances were still issued from Rome. How could one suppose of them that they were kept a secret from the pagans?

[5] *Cod. Theod.* xvi. 2. 4; E. Stein, *Geschichte des spätröm. Reiches*, i, 1928, 149.

These unexpected and unheard-of favours assured him, as a matter of course, the devoted support and acclamation of the clergy. 'At one stroke he had won over the bishops. For ten long years they had resisted every threat and every danger; but evidences of favour were irresistible.'[1] But these favours were, indeed, unexampled. Probably before the end of the year A.D. 312 Constantine exempted the clergy—with the exception of the sectarians—from the heavy financial obligations of the municipal administration.[2] Quite apart from this he, at a later date, assured them maintenance at the public expense.[3] The State finances were so demoralized that the late Roman Emperors only very reluctantly determined on such releases from the burden of taxation. Such reliefs were only granted to trades and professions of public utility. By his action, then, the Emperor recognized Christianity as an organization of public usefulness. As he actually says in his edict, the clergy exercise an activity that benefits the State and must, therefore, be rewarded with privileges.[4]

As early as A.D. 314 Constantine placed the teams of the imperial post at the disposal of such bishops as intended to attend the Synod of Arles. It was a privilege hitherto only granted to imperial messengers and high officials.[5] Later came edicts entrusting the clergy with functions of a directly public character. One such ordinance, of A.D. 318, assigned to the jurisdiction of the bishops the same validity as that of the magistrates; it could be invoked at will by the parties to a

[1] G. Boissier, *La Fin du paganisme*, i⁸. 57.
[2] Euseb. *H.E.* x. 6 and 7. *Cod. Theod.* xvi. 2. i. 2–7. The other authorities may be found in Seeck, *Geschichte d. Untergangs der antiken Welt*, iii², 513, on p. 328, l. 26. N. H. Baynes, op. cit. 68 f., puts back a little the dates of Seeck, *Regesten der Kaiser und Päpste*, 1919, 55, 151, 161. Seeck, however, in *Gesch. d. Unt. d. ant. Welt*, i⁴. 136, writes: 'certainly one of his first acts after the victory was to free the Christian priesthood from all municipal burdens'. See also G. Wissowa, *Religion und Kult der Römer²*, 1912, 500. Here, too, the question forces itself on us: did the pagans really know nothing about it?
[3] Le Nain de Tillemont, *Hist. des Empereurs*, iv. 181.
[4] Euseb. *H.E.* x. 7. 1 (p. 891. 7 Schwartz), which is always being quoted.
[5] Euseb. *H.E.* x. 5. 21 ff. *Appendix Optati Milev.* no. III, ed. Ziwsa = H. v. Soden, 'Urkunden', S. 17 f. Was this also a 'secret'?

case.[1] And let us not forget that every tiny city had its bishop. A second favour, of similar character, was the new form of emancipation of slaves (A.D. 321). Manumission by the clergy in church was placed on a level with manumission by the magistrates.[2] It was a law of Constantine that took the first step towards imposing on the pagan world the calendar of Church festivals. This law arranges for the keeping holy of the Sunday.[3] The Christian day of rest fell, of course, on the *dies Solis*, the day dedicated to the very popular Sun-god. But that fact does not make the step 'neutral'.[4] All days of the week were assigned to their special deities, and any other choice might equally well be called an 'ambiguous gesture'. But there was nothing in Sol or in any other pagan god to justify the Sunday rest, which is based on the authority of the Bible.[5] Christianity had long been holding its regular services on the Sunday.[6] Eusebius,

[1] *Cod. Theod.* i. 27. 1; O. Seeck, *Regesten*, 57; F. Martroye, *Bull. Soc. nat. des Ant. de France*, 1911, 17 ff.; V. Bušek, *Zeitschr. d. Savigny-Stiftung, Kanon. Abt.* xxviii, 1939, 453 ff.; J. Vogt, *Festschr. f. L. Wenger*, ii, 1944, 123 ff.

[2] *Cod. Theod.* iv. 7. 1; O. Seeck, *Regesten*, 61 and 171; Ed. Schwartz, *Göttinger gel. Nachrichten*, 1904, 536; C. Dupont, *Les Constitutions de Constantin et le droit privé au début du IVe s.*, 1937, 42 ff.; J. Vogt, op. cit. 123 f.; G. Mor, *Rivista di storia del diritto romano*, 1928, 80 ff.

[3] See Note 15, p. 130.

[4] Euseb. *Vita Const.* 4. 18, mentions the law, recorded in *Cod. Theod.* ii. 8. 1, *Cod. Just.* iii. 12. 2, with the comment that in the spirit of Christian teaching it devotes the day to the Lord. The law itself only says that it is unworthy of the day of 'Sol' to spend it in wrangling and quarrelling: 'Sicut indignissimum videbatur diem Solis veneratione sui celebrem altercantibus iurgiis et noxiis partium contentionibus occupari, ita gratum et iucundum est eo die quae sunt maxime votiva conpleri. Atque ideo emancipandi et manumittendi die festo cuncti licentiam habeant et super his rebus acta non prohibeantur.'

[5] J. Geffcken, *Der Ausgang des griechisch-römischen Heidentums*, 1920, 94; H. Lietzmann, *Geschichte d. alten Kirche*, iii, 1938, 132; A. Piganiol, op. cit. 129, who assigns it a philosophic origin. See also W. Weber, *Archiv für Religionswissenschaft*, xix, 1919, 330 ff.; J. Vogt, *Festschr. f. L. Wenger*, ii, 1944, 146 f.

[6] See Justin, *Apol.* i. 67. 7, &c. But it was quite another matter when the Church clothed the day of the Redeemer in the symbolical glory of the Sun: F. J. Dölger, *Sol salutis*[2], 1925, 164.

then, is only telling the truth when he says that the Emperor, because of his Christian views, raised Sunday to the rank of a festival. Nor can we doubt that Constantine himself observed the festival with the greatest reverence and caused it to be so observed by his army.[1]

There was another line along which Constantine pursued the task of bringing Church and State closer together. He called Christians in ever-increasing numbers to the higher administrative posts of the Empire. When we find the Synod of Arles (A.D. 314) regulating the position of Christian governors from the point of view of Church discipline (Canon 7), the intention obviously is to get over the abrupt refusal of State service, hitherto customary, and to ease the position of the new men whom Constantine nominated to such posts; they must have been available in large numbers. By the decision of the synod, such governors must do nothing to infringe Church discipline, must not take part in the acts of pagan sacrifice, which, till then, had been bound up with the functions of office. The revolutionary nature of this decision was bound to be peculiarly apparent when the Christian governors, on the 3rd of January and other days of imperial festival, failed to perform the sacrifices for the Emperor, which had been regarded as the pledge of the loyalty of the subjects, and did not compel others to perform them. Among the first Christian dignitaries under Constantine we find his later confidant, Ablabius.[2]

So far we have merely been chronicling a series of symptoms which show that Constantine, in his section of the Empire, was fully in earnest with his bold plan[3] of fitting the Church as a

---

[1] Euseb. *Vita Const.* 4. 18–19, ibid. 20: The prayer prescribed for the pagan soldiers is in itself purely 'neutral', a sigh breathed up to the Lord of Heaven, such as any man might utter; but this is not at all what has been supposed; Constantine does not disguise his own belief, but either will not or dare not make his pagan army Christian against its will. See also Sozom. *H.E.* i. 8. 11–12. For the Christian explanation see, for example, K. Müller, *Kirchengeschichte*, i², 1929, 357; N. H. Baynes, *C.A.H.*, xii, 1939, 694, &c.

[2] H. v. Soden, *Urkunden*, no. 14, p. 18, gives the name in the form 'Aelafius' = 'Aflafius'. Baynes, Raleigh Lecture (1930), 76, thinks that he is not the same as Ablabius.

[3] Ed. Schwartz, *Kaiser Konstantin und die christliche Kirche²*, 1936, 71; the theme is treated by many others.

great driving-wheel into the mechanism of absolutism. When, immediately after taking over the African provinces, he tried most energetically to settle the Donatist schism, he had already in view that dream of a mighty consolidation of forces[1] at which he was continually aiming in all his reforms of the order of State and army. He will not allow the mighty organism of the Faithful to be splintered, in order that it may be the more effective as a pillar of his Empire. That is why he is always pushing himself forward as negotiator and mediator in all cases of friction and division in the Church, and thereby over-burdening his administration and police with the execution of his decisions on Church policy. Yet he is always submitting himself to the clergy, and he openly confesses as much in his letter to the Synod of Arles. He goes out of his way to assevere rate that he is the instrument of the Church ; and the result is that the aims of the Church more and more take him captive. And the true aim of the Church, as soon as it ceased to be intimidated, must end in the endeavour to gain that exclusive right to a religious philosophy which results from the teaching of the Bible. Constantine's path, therefore, tended more and more to take this direction—the annihilation of paganism.

Together with the thought of a Christian world-empire must have arisen in Constantine the thought of a Christian world-capital. The obvious solution to the problem must have seemed to be the christianization of Rome herself. The statue which proclaimed that Constantine had set Rome free through the wondrous power of Christ might be pointed to as a prelude to the attempt. The Seat of Peter enjoyed a remarkable reputation in the Roman world, and the grand Roman past still cast on the venerable shrines of the nation the gleam of its magic light. Long after Constantine, those shrines still com-manded the inner parts of the city—not a single Christian church had yet ventured in. Constantine was, in fact, forced to reckon with the sensibilities of the pagan circles in Rome ; we see this in the fact that, although in the decades just before

---

[1] This comes out most clearly in Constantine's letter addressed to Pope Miltiades: Euseb. *H.E.* x. 5. 20. For a criticism of the Acts relating to the Donatists, see O. Seeck, *Geschichte des Untergangs d. ant. Welt*, iii², 318 ff., and N. H. Baynes, op. cit. 75 ff.

him the more important Church buildings were steadily drawing closer in towards the centre,[1] under him the advance came to a standstill. He was content to erect his magnificent Church buildings along the main lines of approach to the city; only the Lateran Basilica passed the city wall.[2] But, beyond doubt, he enveloped the hearth of the Apostle Princes with the golden gleam of an imperial residence, and all in order to be able to keep Rome as the ideal centre of his Empire, Christian as it now was.

In the course of his first stay in Rome Constantine had made a present to Miltiades, Bishop of Rome, of the palace of the family of the Laterani, the property of his wife. The papal household thus attained a truly princely magnificence.[3] At the same time the Emperor must have arranged for the building of the Lateran Basilica; for, as A. Piganiol acutely observed and as H. v. Schoenebeck has further worked out, all the endowments made over to this Church are in Italy. From this it follows that, at the time of the gift, neither the Balkan districts, won by Constantine in A.D. 314, which were able to contribute possessions to the later foundation of the Lateran Baptistery, nor the Eastern provinces, won in A.D. 324, which were brought in to help endow the Basilica of Peter of the Vatican, were yet in the hands of Constantine.[4] We have not only the lists of the landed possessions bestowed on the Lateran Basilica, but we have also the authentic record of the fabulous wealth of gold and silver which formed its treasure.[5] Such a dazzling equipment could only have been intended for the adornment of the Christian capital. This was, indeed, the first occasion that Constantine transferred the apparatus of imperial display to a Christian shrine; we can grasp this clearly in one detail—the use of the imperial canopy above the throne.[6] On the Cross of gold, given to the Lateran Basilica, the inscription[7] declares

[1] H. v. Schoenebeck, 'Beiträge zur Religionspolitik des Maxentius und Constantin', *Klio*, Beih. xliii, 1939, 87 ff.
[2] Ibid.   [3] See Note 16, p. 130.   [4] See Note 17, p. 130.
[5] *Liber pontif.* i, pp. 172 ff. Duchesne = pp. 52 ff. ed. Mommsen.
[6] A. Alföldi in *Mitteilungen d. Deutschen Archäol. Instituts, römische Abt.* l, 1935, 132.
[7] *Liber pontif.* i, p. 176 Duchesne. Cf. also R. Delbrück, *Die Antike*, viii, 1932, 20 and id., *Antike Porphyrwerke*, 1932, 28.

expressly that the Emperor is minded to pass on the glory of the imperial Court to the chief Church of the capital.[1] Clearer evidence than that of all these details about the intentions of Constantine is given by the demands which he made on the great architect to whom he entrusted the planning of the basilica.

It appears, then, that, before the Lateran Basilica, no single Christian church on the grand scale existed and that the opportunity was now for the first time offered to plan and execute an arrangement of the Church interior according to the laws of architectural art, while keeping in view the requirements of ritual and the need to seat great masses of believers. The magnificent building that rose on the site of the Lateran became the model for all succeeding sacred buildings of the Christian Church. It became *mater et caput omnium ecclesiarum*.[2] In this mighty creation of art that reflected the sanctity of the Christian Empire, the omnipotent Emperor set a worthy rival by the side of the Capitol.[3]

[1] It is certainly a fact that the idea of letting the house of God shine in all the splendour of Empire crops up on all sides; Eusebius, for example, uses for the Basilica of Tyre the description τὸν δὲ βασίλειον οἶκον. But in the case of Rome, the words are not merely intended symbolically.

[2] Cf. G. Rodenwaldt, *C.A.H.* xii, 1939, 569; Th. Klauser, *Vom Heroon zur Märtyrerbasilika*, 1942, 24.

[3] Scholars who have drawn the portrait of a Constantine, still after 28 October A.D. 312 neutral and double-dealing, must not resent the question again and again presented to them: did Constantine really have the Lateran Basilica built 'in secret'?

V

THE FIRST PERIOD OF THE INDEPENDENT RELI-
GIOUS POLICY OF CONSTANTINE: FROM THE
BATTLE OF THE MULVIAN BRIDGE TO THE
SECOND PERIOD OF TENSION WITH LICINIUS.

b. *The attitude of Constantine to the pagans*

IN the autumn of A.D. 312 the Christian community was still rejoicing in the confirmation of tolerance; soon it could begin to enjoy its advance to equality of rights and, then again, bask blissfully in the sun of imperial favour. But it could not yet even dream of destroying paganism. The Faithful were, of course, excluded by their creed from worshipping any god but One. In the iron refusal of the martyrs to take any part in pagan sacrifice it was the complete lack of religious toleration that was the decisive factor. It was only the oppressed state of the Church that denied this feeling any active effect. Constantine, with his logic, crystal-clear, could probably foresee the gathering clouds of later developments. But the Church had long been demanding nothing but toleration for itself, while preaching toleration for all. Let us listen to the words of Lactantius, written just before these events—that Lactantius whose thoughts ran so close to those of the victor of the Mulvian Bridge:

'But religion is the one field in which freedom has pitched her tent. For religion is, first and foremost, a matter of free will, and no man can be forced under compulsion to adore what he has no will to adore. He may perhaps make a hypocritical show of so doing, but will it he cannot. If, then, anyone, out of fear of the tools of torture or vanquished by the torture itself, finally assents to the accursed pagan sacrifice, he never acts of his own free will, as compulsion was involved. As soon as opportunity offers and he recovers his freedom, he comes back to his God and begs with tears for forgiveness, doing penance for that which he did, not of his own free will, which he did not possess, but under the compulsion to which he was submitted, and the Church will not withhold its forgiveness. What good can you do, then, if you defile the body, but cannot break the will?'[1]

[1] See Note 18, p. 130.

The pagans, then, can hardly have feared that lightning would strike them out of a clear sky.

They had all the less reason to fear, because the basis of the agreements of Milan was that very toleration that we have been studying. It assured, in express terms, to every religion the free exercise of its cult, in order that thus the most diverse gods might offer their protection to the Emperor and his subjects.[1] As a result of this way of thinking, no *immediate* change of attitude towards the paganism of the Empire took place. The policy which the Emperor adopted towards the pagans is sharply defined in a group of monuments which have been saved from loss by the durability of their material and the greatness of their numbers, while most other evidences of this original favouring of paganism, which was so soon to perish, have fallen victims to time or were suppressed in silence by after generations. This group is represented by the coins. On the bronze, struck at Rome and other mints as well,[2] after the overthrow of Maxentius, the most characteristic types are Mars, Hercules, and Genius Populi Romani (we must not forget that sacrifice to him was one of the sharpest tests in the persecutions), and also the invincible Sun-god, the companion of the Emperor. Beside the Christian references which are quite sporadic on the fine occasional issues of gold and silver,[3] struck in Ticinum for the imperial Decennalia, Sol Invictus is strongly represented, and, among a mass of divine personifications—Fortune, Fides, Concordia, Pax—Mars does not fail to appear. In A.D. 317, on the occasion of the proclamation of the new Caesars and heirs, Jupiter Conservator and, even more so, the type of Sol Invictus appear on the reverses of the small bronze.[4] Not until A.D. 320–1, when the settlement with Licinius, who had relapsed into paganism, was casting its shadows before, do the figures of the old gods quite disappear

[1] See Note 19, p. 131.

[2] O. Voetter, *Numismatische Zeitschrift*, l, 1917, 29 ff.; li, 1918, 186 f.; J. Maurice, *Numismatique Constantinienne*, i. 202 f., 218 ff., 283 ff., 309 ff. and ii. 38, 94 ff., 124 ff., 232 ff., 327, 435; H. v. Schoenebeck, op. cit. 35 ff., 134 ff.

[3] A. Alföldi, *J.R.S.* xxii, 1932, 19 ff. and *Pisciculi*, 4.

[4] O. Voetter, op. cit.; J. Maurice, op. cit. i. 218 ff.; H. v. Schoenebeck, op. cit. 38.

from the coins. This is clear evidence that eight short years had sufficed Constantine to shake off the fetters of those decisions at Milan which he had, of his own accord, put on.

There is one fact that has already struck scholars. Whilst the pagan gods who had survived through that initial spirit of tolerance, and whilst the abstract personifications, represented as deities, one by one disappear from the types of Constantine, Sol Invictus not only appears most regularly of them all, but also lasts the longest over the whole domain of the Emperor and in all his mints. But there is nothing to surprise us in this; the pagans, as we have already seen, had an attachment of special loyalty to the god.[1] But, quite apart from this, it appears that the Emperor was personally deeply devoted to Sol, and, further, that he could not at once break all the threads that bound him to that world of thought in which he had been born and bred.

Many varied attempts have been made to explain this phenomenon—none particularly successful. The attitude of Constantine was consciously Christian, as we have already observed from many telling examples. We cannot, therefore, possibly assume in him the kind of advanced syncretism, the religion of the melting-pot, that we observe in the pagans and the gnostic sects of the time. It was a syncretism that would have drowned Christianity in the swamps of polytheism,[2] or have dissolved it in the thin mists of Neoplatonic henotheism.[3] In Constantine, with his superior consistency, there is no trace of cleavage in his religious consciousness.[4] Again, the important

---

[1] N. H. Baynes, *J.R.S.* xxv, 1935, 86, rightly emphasizes that it is essential to 'distinguish between Constantine's personal belief and his action as the ruler both of pagans and Christians'.

[2] Among typical representatives of this view are, for example, Th. Keim, *Der Übertritt Constantins d. Gr. zum Christentum*, 1862, 41 ff.; Th. Zahn, *Konstantin der Grosse und die Kirche*, 1876; L. Salvatorelli, *Rivista storica italiana*, xliv, N.S. v, 1927, 169 f.; id., *Ricerche religiose*, iv, 1928, 289 ff. (and in his other works); H. Grégoire, *Revue de l'Université de Bruxelles*, xxxvi, 1930/1931, 231 ff., &c.

[3] V. Duruy, *Histoire des Romains*, vii, 1885, 36 ff.; P. Batiffol, *La Paix Constantinienne*, 3rd edition, 1914, 188 ff.

[4] As J. Maurice, for example, assumed: *Comptes-rendus de l'Académie des Inscriptions et Belles-Lettres*, 1909, 165 ff. and 1910, 101 ff.

role played by Sol cannot be eliminated by the supposition that Constantine, down to A.D. 324,[1] was forced to take account of Licinius. Had that been the case, Jupiter and his companions would not have vanished from the coinage while Sol remained. Nor is it credible that Sol, on the coins of Constantine, serves as a connecting link between the second Flavian dynasty and its founders and represents the memory of his great forebears.[2] When Constantine wished to induce belief in the descent of his family from the great Pannonian general or work on the emotions of his subjects towards the dynasty, he placed the portraits of Claudius II, Constantius Chlorus, and Herculius on his coins at various times between A.D. 314 and 324. Again, the identification of Sol with Christ cannot have been the reason why the Sun-god became the constant companion of the Emperor.[3] Had that been the case, it would have been expressed by one or another symbol, generally intelligible at the time. But that was not so. In the Sol of the *Soli invicto comiti Augusti nostri* on coins of Constantine men could not possibly see anyone but the imperial patron,[4] who had been so widely advertised as such from the third century onwards, the invincible Sun-god, identified with Mithras. All the explanations that I have rejected either aim by such interpretation at taking the force out of testimonies disagreeable to them, or at calling the Christian faith of Constantine into question because of these survivals of paganism in him— an unjustifiable procedure.

Yet, after all, the logic of Constantine's progress is quite easy to understand if we neither eliminate nor over-estimate those limitations of the thought of the later Rome as we find them in him. It was very difficult for the ancients to conceive

---

[1] As, for example, N. H. Baynes, Raleigh Lecture (1930), 95, thinks possible.

[2] Baynes, ibid. 97, following J. Maurice, who declares the four protecting deities of the Tetrarchy to be symbols which actually determine rank, exactly defining the position of each Emperor. Baynes overworks the idea. Maurice also thinks that the coins struck in the several parts of the Empire for the other colleagues were, quite systematically, provided with portraits of the ruler of the section of the Empire in each case in question: a simplification of the same kind.

[3] N. H. Baynes, op. cit. 97 ff.

[4] *Mitteilungen d. D. Arch. Inst., röm. Abt.* xlix, 1934, 43 ff., &c.

that there could be only one god. Even the Churchmen believed in the living actuality of the pagan gods—only with
a difference; they regarded them, not as good spirits, but as
evil demons.[1] We have already emphasized the fact that, in
the view of the Edict of Milan, Christ is only the most powerful
among many gods.[2] We can advance farther towards an
understanding if we consider the deep influence of Neoplatonic
philosophy. In absorbing the conceptions of the Sun-god with
the rest of the popular religions, it set Sol on the throne of the
universe and made it easy to suppose that this supreme being
was none other than the Almighty of the Christians.[3] The
summa divinitas, the nameless supreme deity of the Edict of
Toleration of Milan, assuredly bears the stamp of the style of
this philosophic deism.[4] Even at the end of his life, Constantine had not been able to free himself from the influence of
a few Neoplatonic philosophers, such as Hermogenes and
Sopatros; and these gentlemen were, of course, priests and
magicians rather than scholars. This connexion of solar
monotheism with the Christian Almighty, and so with Christ,
may have been a bond of union between them. Such muddled
combinations of quite distinct forms of monotheism were all
the easier, because the Church, on its side, had long been using
the comparison of Christ with the Sun as an instructive symbol,
naming Him 'Sun of Truth', 'Sun of Resurrection', 'Sun of
Salvation', and thus admitting the influence of the cult of Sol.[5]
There were two bridges, then, by which Constantine could,
with a good conscience, cross over to a toleration of Sol beside
the Redeemer.

[1] See, meanwhile, for example, M. Vogelstein, *Kaiser-idee, Rom-idee*, 1930,
57, n. 4. We shall discuss the point in full in the second part of our volume
on Valentinian I. Of course it was not only the Christian Church and Constantine that were convinced of the existence of the pagan gods; the Emperor
Galerius, for example, believed, like all his contemporaries, that the Almighty
of the Christians actually existed; see the quotation in Note 19, p. 131.
[2] See the remarks of G. Boissier, op. cit. i[8]. 45 f.
[3] Cf. for example, K. Müller, *Historische Zeitschrift*, cxl, 1929, 263.
[4] See Note 20, p. 131.
[5] H. Usener, *Das Weihnachtsfest*[2], 1911; Fr. J. Dölger, *Sol salutis*[2], 1925;
H. v. Schoenebeck, op. cit. 24 ff.; Fr. J. Dölger, *Die Sonne der Gerechtigkeit
und der Schwarze*, 1919, 83 ff.

But whatever the motive for Constantine's continued loyalty to Sol even after his vision—whether regard for his pagan subjects or truth to his own earlier inclinations—he was bound very soon to realize that his conduct in this respect was inconsistent with his whole attitude towards Christianity. He began to aim at repairing the defect. How he did so the coins will show.

In A.D. 317, when the Emperors of East and West appointed their sons Caesars and heirs, there appears on the coins of Licinius I and II the figure of Jupiter the preserver, while the reverses of Constantine are dedicated to the 'invincible Sungod'. But, on one type of his sons, Sol is represented with the legend *Claritas Reipublicae*. The Sun is no longer a god, but simply the glorious fame of the State; and this glory is not really referred to the State, but to the young prince shown on the obverse; we find similar uses for the Emperors of the Tetrarchy.[1] A little later, this allegory of the Sun used to glorify the Emperor, this *Claritas Reipublicae*,[2] appears on the gold of Constantine himself and his son of the same name. In this connexion it is most remarkable how often Eusebius compares his Emperor to the star that sheds light and blessed warmth abroad,[3] and even more frequent is the similar practice in a Christian poet who writes in Latin, Optatianus Porphyrius.[4] The imperial patron certainly took delight in such comparisons; they may even have been made at his direct suggestion. There was nothing new in such similes. Even before the monarchy, the flattery of the East was bathing the

[1] H. Usener, *Das Weihnachtsfest*[2], 1911, 362.

[2] The dates in H. v. Schoenebeck, op. cit., 140.

[3] Joh. Straub, *Vom Herrscherideal der Spätantike*, 1939, 132 gives the relevant passages.

[4] An illustration of the 'neutralized' conception of *Sol comes* is given by Opt. Porf. *carm.* 12. 1 ff., especially 6: 'sol tibi felices faciet spes perpete nutu' (A.D. 324); *carm.* 18. 25 f.: 'lumine muriceo venerandus dux erit, ut sol, legibus ut Iani teneas avus orbe tribunal'. Cf. also *carm.* 8. 1: 'accipe picta novis elegis, lux aurea mundi', &c.; *carm.* 11. 13: 'lux unica mundi' (A.D. 324/325); *carm.* 14. 2: 'lux pia terrarum' (from the same epoch); *carm.* 15. 10: 'lux pia Romulidum'; *carm.* 15. 14: 'lux aurea Romae'; *carm.* 17. 15: 'aurea lux vatum'; *carm.* 18. 2: 'luce tua signes fastos sine limite consul'; *carm.* 19. 2: 'Constantine, decus mundi, lux aurea saecli'; *carm.* 19. 12: 'Romula lux'. And it all applies to the emperor!

generals and envoys of the Republic in the rays of the Sun,[1] and then, under the Empire, Sol was made to sacrifice his sovereign remoteness and sink, so to speak, to be the lackey of the Emperor, *comes Augusti*. This long process of declension made it all the easier for Constantine to degrade the sun till he became the source of his own glory. His own earlier worship of Sol, thus reinterpreted, could be represented as a cult that could give no offence to Christians. Usener has already observed that the legend *Claritas Reipublicae* round the figure of Sol is a deliberate attempt to obscure Constantine's own earlier relationship to a patron deity.[2] The Court, naturally, did not restrict this 'disinfection' of the Emperor's sun-worship to the coins, but extended it to paintings and statues now lost.[3] And such was its success that. in the last period of Constantine's life, the Emperor's statue with the inscription 'To Constantine all glorious as the Sun' could be erected in the imperial capital.[4] But Constantine carefully avoided any suggestion of Sun-worship. He exchanged the imperial title *Invictus*, 'Invincible', for the epithet *Victor*, 'Victorious', so that none might be reminded of the *Sol invictus* from whose name his ancestors had taken their title of *invictus*.[5] We might still, however, raise one question. Was this conversion of the Sun into the lordly source of light of the Sun-Emperor only begun in A.D. 317? It may be so, but we do not know for certain. In any case, Constantine had upset the platform of his own Milan decree with astonishing speed, and erased from his own soul the little that yet remained of his original religious personality.[6]

Constantine found himself confronted by millions of pagans,

[1] See the passages quoted in Fr. J. Dölger, *Sol salutis*[2], 1925, 396 f., 402; many more might easily be added.
[2] H. Usener, *Das Weihnachtsfest*[2], 1911, 364.
[3] Cf. the base of a statue from Termessos in Pisidia, with the inscription Κωνσταντείνῳ ⟨νέῳ⟩ Ἡλίῳ παντεπόπτῃ, quoted from Fr. Cumont, *Textes et monuments*, i. 290; Fr. J. Dölger, op. cit. 66 ff.
[4] See Note 21, p. 131.
[5] See, for example, A. Piganiol, op. cit. 146; J. Gagé, *Revue d'histoire et de philosophie religieuse*, 1933, 393; for the title *victor* many documents could be quoted. Cf., for example, Ed. Schwartz, *Göttinger gel. Nachrichten*, 1904, 388, no. 25; 394, no. 8, &c.
[6] See Note 22, p. 132.

but among those vast masses there was scarcely a single group that dared to defy the imperial might. The energies of the city population, owing to much earlier blood-letting and to the slackness of peace, had fallen asleep; while, in the provinces, the ceaseless waste of continuous wars had destroyed the vital forces of those who carried the self-consciousness of Romans, in the course of their service of twenty-five or thirty years' duration. More than this, the fearful crisis of the third century had everywhere broken up the civil layers of the population, and all that had survived succumbed to the screw of taxation.

But the opposition of the army, on the other hand, might have been alarming. Those elements, however, in which the old feelings of national patriotism remained alive, that is to say the Celtic and Illyrian soldiers in their masses and their non-commissioned officers, had been wiped out one by one in the wars of the third century. Already among the corps that had enjoyed the chief reputation in earlier generations appeared the African robber-peoples, with their short arrows stuck in their wiry hair, and, beside them, the Syrian and Mesopotamian archers and the allied detachments of German and other foreign peoples that fought under the leadership of their own chieftains. And now this Germanization of the army advanced with alarming speed. These peoples could feel no interest in the fate of Jupiter Optimus Maximus, only in their own religious ideas, interwoven with foreign superstitions of every kind. This wild medley of mercenaries was dominated by the fear of enchantment or the intoxication of the Eastern mysteries—so far as they had not yet been conquered by Christianity. We can hardly suppose them capable of feeling that Roman loyalty and discipline, ideas relatively unfamiliar to them, depended on the retention of traditional ceremonies. Constantine, who was very tender of their susceptibilities in religious matters, was the ablest general of his age and scattered his gold among them with a liberal hand. From them he had nothing to fear.

In those days, when there was no violent destruction of sacred sites to excite the bitterness of such pagan subjects as still clung to their gods, or kindle the fanaticism of the inhabitants of particular districts, there was only one social group capable of grasping the threatening danger in its full magnitude, once the resistance to Christianity of the military circles of the Balkans, from which Constantine himself sprang, had died out with the bankruptcy of the great persecutions. That group was the Senate, which, with its great traditions, its prestige still unbroken by its ousting from leadership, and its enormous wealth, could still present some kind of a bold front against the Emperor. It was into this age-old citadel that the Emperor entered on the 29th of October A.D. 312: let us follow him.

After the praetorian guard, the mainstay of the throne of Maxentius, had bled to death in the battle of the Tiber, Constantine was welcomed in Rome with general relief.[1] The popularity of his predecessor had already begun to totter. The Senate had not even taken any prominent part in his proclamation,[2] and, gladly as they may have listened at first to his glorification of the great past of Rome, he incurred their hostility later when he laid heavy burdens on their shoulders.[3] Moreover, Maxentius did not rest especially on senatorial support. Not once in his six years of power did he confer the distinction of the ordinary consulship on its members, not once did he praise them on his coins. Perhaps he may even have sought in his favours to the Christian masses of the lower orders a counterpoise to the aristocracy.[4] But he failed to win the enthusiasm of the city mob, too. It had suffered terribly from famine, for the African corn-fleet had been prevented by the pretender, Alexander, A.D. 308–11, from delivering its normal load. The unrest of the 'plebs' broke out once in bloody street-fighting, the suppression of which demanded thousands of victims and only served to heighten resentment.[5] And so there was sincerity both in the rejoicings of the senators,

---

[1] Lately treated by, for example, M. Besnier, *L'Empire romain de l'avènement des Sévères au concile de Nicée*, 1937, 360.

[2] E. Groag, *RE*. xiv. 2423.

[3] E. Groag, *RE*. xiv. 2417, 2423 ff., 2454, 2456; E. Stein, *Geschichte des spätröm. Reiches*, i, 1928, 192, &c.

[4] Cf. Ed. Schwartz, *Göttinger gel. Nachr.* 1904, 532.

[5] E. Groag, *RE*. xiv. 2465 f.

who rushed to meet the victor, and in the choruses of acclamation from the 'plebs' that surged through the streets.[1] The
festal procession once more moved up to the Capitol, as had
for so many centuries been the custom of victorious generals in
their triumphs. It would have been wellnigh impossible for
Constantine to insult the enthusiasm of Rome by making his
way straight to the Palatine without first sacrificing to Jupiter,
Best and Greatest[2]—however uncomfortable he may have felt
in so doing.

Constantine treated the Senate with perfect respect.[3] He
still nominated its members to posts in the priestly colleges of
the old religion, and he did this in his capacity as chief of the
pontifices; for he still retained the rank of *pontifex maximus*,
which all rulers since Augustus had reserved for themselves.
Thus he remained the head of the pagan religion of the State,
and, if he let the oversight of the ancient rites be exercised by
a *pro-magister*, that made no real difference. The *pontifices*,
augures, and *quindecimviri* could still fulfil their duties un-
changed, as could also the *haruspices*, the searchers of the
entrails,[4] who for long generations continued to make their
customary reports to the Court when lightning struck any
public building in Rome.[5]

How completely reliable the Senate was, from the standpoint
of Constantine, appears from the fact that he took again into
his service[6] senators who had held high positions under his
defeated opponent, and that he succeeded in putting an end to

[1] E. Stein, op. cit., i. 140, note 3; E. Groag, *RE*. xiv. 2481.
[2] Joh. Straub, *Vom Herrscherideal der Spätantike*, 1939, 98 and 261, n. 110,
takes a different view; with him agrees J. Vogt, *Zeitschr. f. Kirchengesch.*
1942, 174 f. But the passages quoted (*Paneg.* xii. 19. 3 and Zosimus ii. 29. 5)
do not refer to this event, or not to this date at all. We must, also, not forget
that not before A.D. 326 did Constantine venture in Rome to give expression
to his displeasure at such a festal procession; and, even when he did so, he
had actually set out himself for a pagan temple.
[3] *Cod. Theod.* xv. 14. 4; cf. O. Seeck, Savigny's *Zeitschr. f. Rechtsgesch.*,
romanistische Abt. x, 207 and id., *Geschichte des Untergangs der ant. Welt*, i⁴,
136 and 499.
[4] Zosim. ii. 29. 1: ἐχρῆτο δὲ ἔτι καὶ τοῖς πατρίοις ἱεροῖς.
[5] *Cod. Theod.* xvi. 10. 1; V. Schultze, *Zeitschr. f. Kirchengesch.* viii, 1886,
522 f.; cf. also below, pp. 75 ff.
[6] E. Groag, *RE*. xiv. 2447, 2481; O. Seeck, *Gesch. d. Unt.* i⁴. 137.

the widespread mischief of denunciations.[1] For the moment
he felt the need for that legislative machinery of the old
Republic. After all, the Senate was the only body that could,
with any show of legality, invest him with the rank of first
Augustus, in place of Maximin Daza, who was still ruling in the
East. The importance of this position had been brought out
by the frictions in Diocletian's system of four rulers.[2] It was
a position that could not merely satisfy Constantine's ambition, but could also assist him on his path to sole rule.

All too soon he was presented with the opportunity to use
the Senate as a tool in delicate matters of political importance. There is no doubt that he prevailed on the Senate to
declare Maxentius a tyrant. By this act of *damnatio memoriae*
the acts of the tyrant lost all their validity. All indications
suggest[3] that Constantine again made use of the Senate, that
purely nominal bearer of constitutional rights long since
overthrown, to condemn the memory of the quarrelsome
father-in-law, Maximian Herculius, whom he had put to death.
In this way his conduct towards him could be represented in a
satisfactory and reasonable light.

This relationship of mutual dependency explains another
fact. After the taking of Rome, those verbose phrases about
the fall of the capricious tyrant and the restoration of the
ancient Republican liberty, which he had oppressed,[4] did not
only ring loud from the lips of the flatterers of the victor, but
were taken over and broadcast by the official propaganda.
Writers and rhetoricians, Christian and pagan alike, repeat
these flowers of speech in the old Roman style,[5] making Constantine appear as a Republican hero of liberty rushing in to

---

[1] *Cod. Theod.* x. 10. 2.

[2] Lactant. *De mort. pers.* 44. 11. Characteristic examples of the effects of
this passion for titles among the Emperors of the Tetrarchy are given by
Lactantius, op. cit. 18. 6; 20. 1; 25. 5; 32. 1; 32. 3; 44. 11. Euseb. *Vita Const.*
1. 18. Constantine himself, in A.D. 324, emphasizes that Diocletian had been
the first in rank: Euseb. *Vita Const.* 2. 51.

[3] Cf. W. Ensslin, *RE.* xiv. 2515 f.

[4] Cf. my remarks in *Zeitschr. f. Numismatik*, xl, 1930, 5 ff.

[5] For example, Euseb. *H.E.* ix. 9. 2; Zonaras, xiii. 1. 7 (3, p. 2 Büttner–
Wobst) and ibid. 1. 13 (ibid., p. 4); Cedrenus, p. 474. 9 Bonn; *Nazar. paneg.*
30. 4–31. 1; Praxagoras, *F. Gr. Hist.* ii B. 948 f.

help his threatened fatherland and save Rome.[1] The same
phraseology is everywhere repeated by the legends of the
monuments that arose to commemorate his victory. The
dedication of the triumphal arch erected in A.D. 315 and still
standing to-day is directed to the *liberator urbis*, the deliverer
who, constitutionally taking up arms, *iustis armis*, takes
revenge on the tyrant and his partisans.[2] The reliefs of the
arch show the senatorial Emperor in senatorial garb in the
midst of the *patres*, the fathers of the city. Other Roman
inscriptions greet him as the restorer of the ancient freedom,
restitutor libertatis publicae;[3] and the classical phrases that
glorify the hero of freedom, who slays the tyrant, recur again
and again on the inscriptions of provincial monuments.[4]

In the phraseology of the Empire, the suppressor of tyranny
and the surety for freedom is the constitutional *princeps*, who
rules in the spirit of ancestral custom. This ideal picture was
spread abroad by the propaganda of the Court on the occasion
of the victory of the Mulvian Bridge, both in the autumn of
A.D. 312 and for many a year after. The larger works of art are
lost, but the coins survive to give us an idea of it. Immediately
after the decisive event, they celebrate Constantine, in the
name of the Senate and people of Rome, as the *optimus
princeps*,[5] as the restorer of Rome,[6] as the new founder of
Roman freedom,[7] to whom the goddess, Roma, in gratitude,
delivers over the rule of the world.[8] The official panegyrics pay
corresponding compliments to the city of Rome: after her
humiliation by the tyrant she has resumed her rule of the world.[9]

---

[1] *Nazar. paneg.* 11. 2 (p. 165 Guil. Baehrens): 'Utrum urbis funestam illam
lacerationem lente ac remisse te laturum putavit' [sc. Maxentius]?

[2] *C.I.L.* vi. 1139 = Dess. 694; H. P. L'Orange, *Der spätantike Bildschmuck
des Konstantinbogens*, 1939, 102.

[3] E.g. *C.I.L.* vi. 1145.

[4] For the dates, see E. Groag, *RE*. xiv. 2481.

[5] With the legend: *SpqR optimo principi*, cf. J. Maurice, *Num. Const.* i,
1907, 203 (no. 4); 286 (no. VII); 287 (no. IX).

[6] *Restitutor Romae*: ibid. 287 (no. VIII). *Recuperatori urb[is] suae*: ibid. ii,
1911, 34 f.; 146 (nos. II–III) and xxx, Pl. V. 2.

[7] *Restitutori libertatis*: *J.R.S.* xxii, 1932, 21 (nos. 17–19).

[8] Ibid., Pl. 2. 15.

[9] *Nazar. paneg.* 31. 2 (p. 180 Guil. Baehrens): 'imperium recepit, quae
servitium sustinebat.'

This great attentiveness towards Rome, this submission before her ancient greatness, on the part of a ruler who, in general, had no enthusiasm for the traditions of the ancient capital, were due, in the first place, to the lessons of a very recent past. Long ago, in A.D. 238, the reaction of the Senate which resulted in its victory over Maximin Thrax, though it did not restore the Senate to mastery, *did* intimidate the soldier-emperors and force them, for half a century, to pay it the deepest reverence. So now, the proclamation of Maxentius, though it had no serious results, yet demonstrated anew that Rome, if pushed on one side, could still defy the Emperor. For six whole years the Eternal City had been an imperial residence and Maxentius had deliberately revived the old Roman national romance,[1] which still retained much more driving power than is commonly supposed to-day.[2]

Constantine spent fully two months in Rome.[3] Apparently he was still there on the 1st of January A.D. 313, to celebrate his entry into office as consul[4] with a brilliant procession and magnificent games. Both panegyrist and official art had long been praising his friendly sociability and his handsome gifts.[5] But, after his victory, Rome ceased for good to be the camp of the praetorian guard[6] and could no longer, therefore, support its political claims by force of arms. Just like the soldier-emperors before him, Constantine refuses to reside in Rome, and, in general, lays no great stress on Italy. We soon find him planning to give this district to Bassianus Caesar, and, again like his immediate predecessors, he only celebrates in this ideal centre of the Empire the festivals of his ten-yearly jubilees,

[1] E. Groag, *RE.* xiv. 2457 ff.

[2] 'From the romantic revival of primitive Roman traditions there was no fresh living force to be drawn', writes Groag, op. cit., 2459. But the future proved the reverse to be the case. We hope to give a study of the Idea of Rome in the last volume of this series of studies.

[3] *Nazar. paneg.* 33. 6: 'bimestris fere cura'.

[4] *Incerti paneg. Constantino Aug. d.* 19. 6 (p. 305 Guil. Baehrens), thus explained by O. Seeck, *Gesch. d. Untergangs d. ant. Welt*, i⁴. 138.

[5] For the reliefs of the Arch of Constantine, relating to this point, see H. P. L'Orange, *Der spätantike Bildschmuck des Konstantinbogens*, 1939, 87 ff., 99 ff.

[6] Aur. Victor, *Caes.* 40. 25. The other sources in E. Stein, op. cit. i. 140.

first in A.D. 315,[1] then again in A.D. 326. But, in spite of all, the *restitutor libertatis* could still for a long time not deny his own first conduct in Rome; not till his dying day could he quite cut the ground away from under the State religion there. While he departed farther and farther from his first Roman programme, the Senate only held on the more obstinately to its religious traditions. This led to friction, the first stages of which we must now trace.

The news that Constantine had joined the Christians, the statue that proclaimed the victory won under the sign of Christ, the Emperor's Christian buildings, like the Lateran Basilica, and other evidences, mostly lost to us to-day, of his continuous endeavour to exalt the Church—all these must have hit the Roman aristocracy amazingly hard. The appetite of the Christians grew with eating. Symptoms of an awakening aggressiveness begin to appear. In the mint of Ticinum, in A.D. 313 and 314, the Cross was regularly used as a series-mark beside Mars and Sol[2]—all with the knowledge of the procurator in charge and the tacit consent of the Court. In view of the magical power attributed to this sign, this meant no innocent piece of symbolism, no individual challenge, but a veritable insult, aimed at depriving the pagan deities of their power to hurt.[3] At the dedication of the Basilica of Tyre, in A.D. 314, the Bishop of Caesarea waxes eloquent on the theme of the Emperor who worships the One True God and His Son, 'spitting in the face of the lifeless idols and laughing to scorn the outworn deceits inherited from our ancestors'.[4] If Con-

---

[1] O. Seeck, *Regesten der Kaiser und Päpste*, 1919, 164; cf. N. H. Baynes, Raleigh Lecture (1930), 79 f., note 51.

[2] J. Maurice, op. cit. 2, p. lviii and 248 f., and H. v. Schoenebeck, op. cit. 37 f.

[3] This was not a variant, used here and there in secret and limited to a very few dies, like the Christian signs, for example, that L. Laffranchi discovered on the issues of the mint of Aquileia under Maxentius. The use of the Cross to neutralize the power of the pagan god comes from the same ideas, drawn from the realm of magic, as Socrates, *H.E.* I. 17, ascribes to Constantine on another occasion; he reports that the Emperor caused a part of the Cross of Christ to be fitted into the statue in Constantinople that represented him in the form of 'Sol'.

[4] Euseb. *H.E.* x. 4. 16.

stantine's Christian policy could already awaken such an echo in distant Palestine, we can readily imagine how much more severely the pagans of Rome must have felt its pressure.[1]

The pillorying of their beliefs as 'outworn deceits inherited from their ancestors' was a terrible affront to them. In the confusion of religions, polytheism, in general, might be breaking up in the melting-pot of syncretism; but the fading of the old conceptions of the gods in the souls of those who carried the Roman traditions could not seriously shake the religion of the State. The faithful performance of the time-honoured ceremonies that was deeply rooted among the ideas of the duty that one owes one's country, *pietas erga rempublicam*, has no real concern with speculations about the gods. These prescribed acts of worship were regarded as something as imperative as Holy Writ—the performance of obligations ordained by their ancestors.

For some long time the political rights of the Senate had been in process of being lopped by the Emperor; the senators had been slowly forfeiting the right to prove themselves in the service of the State. But every Emperor regarded the regular and reverent performance of the *caerimoniae publicae* as his natural duty. It was these very ceremonies of sacrifice that had formed a focus for the persecutions of the Christians. They were acts which attested loyalty to Emperor and State.[2] The emphasis on their importance from this point of view was only increased by the persecutions of Diocletian, and here, if anywhere, there was agreement of sentiment between the leading ranks of the Illyrian soldiers and the conservative noble circles. And was Constantine now about to shatter the foundations of those feelings, on which the salvation of the State depended?

What was the judgement of contemporaries on the matter? 'The greatest of all sins', wrote Diocletian, 'is to upset things that have once been ordained and prescribed by our forefathers, which were shaped by them and still take their

---

[1] Some remarks on the subject may be found in M. Vogelstein, *Kaiseridee—Romidee*, 1930, 51 f.; Ed. Schwartz, *Kaiser Konstantin und die christliche Kirche*[2], 1936, 63 f.

[2] Cf. my arguments in *Klio*, xxxi, 1938, 323 ff.

course.'¹ Galerius emphasizes the same point in his Edict of toleration.²

'Our aim has ever been to effect improvement everywhere in accordance with the old laws and common feelings of the Romans and, therefore, to see to it that the Christians, too, who have abandoned the belief of their fathers, may come to their senses. For—whatever be the reason—such an obstinacy has possessed them, such a stupidity has overpowered them that they will not follow those institutions of the ancients, which their own fathers, it may be, called into being, but have capriciously, at their own whim, made for themselves new laws.'

Against this charge Lactantius, following many other apologists, defends himself: 'But they (the pagans) declare that it is right and proper to punish those who condemn the common creed inherited from our ancestors. What does this imply? If those ancestors were so stupid as to adopt such senseless religions . . . is one to prescribe to us that we shall not follow a true and better religion?'³ And, finally, it was not Julian the Apostate who invented the charge that 'Constantine was a wicked innovator, an upsetter of primaeval laws, of a tradition, sanctified by long use';⁴ no, it was the bearers of the Roman tradition. Eusebius knew full well⁵ why he put into the mouth of Licinius before battle against Constantine such words as these: 'Our country's gods are those whom we adore, because we have inherited their worship from our ancestors of

¹ In the edict about the Manichaeans, *Collectio libr. iuris anteiustiniani*, ed. Krueger, iii, 1890, 187 f. ; 'Maximi enim criminis est retractare quae semel ab antiquis statuta et definita suum statum et cursum tenent ac possident.'
² Lactant. *De mort. pers.* 34. 1–2: '. . . nos quidem volueramus antehac iuxta leges veteres et publicam disciplinam Romanorum cuncta corrigere atque id providere, ut etiam Christiani, qui parentum suorum reliquerant sectam, ad bonas mentes redirent, siquidem quadam ratione tanta eosdem Christianos voluntas invasisset et tanta stultitia occupasset, ut non illa veterum instituta sequerentur, quae forsitan primum parentes eorundem constituerant, sed pro arbitrio suo atque ut isdem erat libitum, ita sibimet leges facerent . . .' = Euseb. *H.E.* viii. 17. 3 ff.
³ Lactant. *Epitome divin. Instit.* l. 1 (*C.S.E.L.* xix, p. 729): 'Sed recte ac merito puniri aiunt eos, qui publicas religiones a maioribus traditas execrantur. Quid? si maiores illi stulti fuerunt in suscipiendis religionibus vanis . . . praescribetur nobis quominus vera et meliora sectemur?'
⁴ Ammian. 21. 10. 8.
⁵ Euseb. *Vita Const.* 2. 5.

old; the leaders of the enemy's army have faithlessly abandoned the traditions of our fathers.'

This way of life, both for individual and State alike, was threatened by the new movement.[1]

The chief characteristic in the conduct of the Senate towards the conqueror of Maxentius is its refusal, prolonged as long as possible, to take any account of his desertion to the side of Christ. Immediately after his victory a golden statue was set up in his honour, in which he was, perhaps, still represented outwardly as a god; if that was the case, it was presumably with the attributes of Sol that he was shown.[2] Probably a college of priests was organized for the divine rulers of his dynasty, the *gens Flavia*, in Rome as well as elsewhere.[3] The Roman mint, along with the other normal types of pagan gods, represents the Emperor as *liberator orbis*, the deliverer of the world, whom the signs of oracles had foretold, thrusting down the lion that symbolizes the principle of evil and, with right hand upstretched, turning heavenward to implore the aid of the gods or of the 'Supreme Being'.[4]

We recognize the same effort as before: the Roman aristocrats and the men of letters of the same mind try to find somewhere in the pantheistic monotheism of the Neoplatonic philosophy a point of contact with the Christian belief of the Emperor in one God. As we have already seen, the programme of Milan actually offered a practical possibility.[5]

The keynote of the Edict of Milan is the *divinus favor*, which helps god-fearing rulers to victory. It is very significant to see how the pagans reinterpret this divine protection—the guiding thought of Constantine, based on his vision. They never

[1] But they were not as slow in thus reacting as, for example, Clifford H. Moore, *Transactions and Proceedings of the American Philological Association*, l, 1919, 126, or M. Vogelstein, *Kaiseridee — Romidee*, 1930, 81 ff., supposes.

[2] See Note 23, p. 132.

[3] Aur. Victor, *Caes.* 40. 28, proves this for Africa, the famous inscription of Hispellum does the same for Umbria; we must assume that Rome set the first example, for such conduct cannot have been suggested from above. See also Mommsen, *Ges. Schriften*, 8. 37 and 44.

[4] I intend to discuss this motif in statuary on the sarcophagi in another article. Cf. my work, *Die Kontorniaten*, 1943, 62 and 117.

[5] In the following passage I am repeating my argument in *Pisciculi*, 14 f.

question the revelation vouchsafed to the Emperor, they do not venture to cast any doubt on the miraculous intervention of God, which the Emperor had announced, but they take no cognizance of its all being the work of Christ and they are at pains to translate the transcendental forces here displayed into terms of their own conceptions.

The Emperor is lord of an Empire that is still officially pagan, he is still himself its head, chief priest of the State religion. He cannot, therefore, prevent the pagans, who still form a majority in the population of the Empire, from regarding their own gods—or, if not them, at least the 'Supreme Being' of Platonism—as the true protectors of an Empire that was still their own.

On the other hand, pagan courtiers, in their official utterances, while emphasizing the part played by the gods in the battle before the gates of Rome, are particularly careful not to mention the old gods by name. They describe the deity in generalizing expressions, capable of corresponding fairly closely to descriptions of the Christian Almighty. These blunted expressions of paganism are the quiet harbingers of the awakening of a violent reaction.[1] Servile as was the attitude of the late Roman to his monarch, the polished pagan rhetorician could still find a tone in which, with all reverence, but also with complete assurance, he could remind his Emperor of what the undying Roman past demanded of him. Such voices kept gaining in strength until finally, after a struggle of seventy years, a pagan aristocrat, as governor of Rome, in an official report, *relatio*, enforced on the notice of the Emperors their obligations to the traditions of the ancient city; and, two decades later, Claudius Claudianus, in melodious and inspiring verse, drummed into the ears of the young Honorius a message that could also penetrate his mind through his eyes—the enchantment of old Rome.

About six months after the brilliant Italian campaign, the author of an official panegyric declared that Constantine had won his victory 'by divine instruction and inspiration', *divino monitus instinctu*.[2] He even ventured to raise the question

[1] See Note 24, p. 132.
[2] *Incerti paneg. Constantino Aug. d.* 11. 4 (p. 298 Guil. Baehrens).

what divinity it was that made Constantine bold to begin a
war from which even the pagan priests had dissuaded him.[1]
But, though he continually emphasized the helpful co-opera-
tion of the gods and the victory 'promised from on High',
divinitus promissa victoria, he supplies no answer to his own
question. He evades it by saying that it is the Emperor's
secret. Instead of answering it, he discusses at great length the
philosophical conception of a single almighty power who
belongs to all—that is to say, not to the Christians only.

'Supreme creator of all things, Who hast chosen to have as many
names as there are languages on earth, what name Thou Thyself pre-
ferrest we may not know—whether in Thee there resides a certain
divine might and divine spirit, with which Thou dost fill the world and
intermingle with all elements and, without any influence from an
external impulse, dost of Thyself come into operation, or whether,
somewhere above all heavens, that might exists, from whence, as from
a high citadel of nature, Thou regardest the work of Thy hands. . . .'[2]

It sounds as if we might be listening to the prelude to the
famous *relatio* of Symmachus.

It was in vain that Constantine had abandoned the platform
of his edict of pantheistic toleration at Milan; the pagans in
A.D. 321 were still refusing to leave it—just as if nothing had
happened in the interval. When every child knew of the
miracle that Christ had wrought in the Italian campaign,[3] a

---

[1] Ibid. 2. 4 (p. 291): 'Quisnam te deus, quae tam praesens hortata est
maiestas, ut . . . contra consilia hominum, contra haruspicum monita ipse
per temet liberandae urbis tempus venisse sentires?' See also ibid. 4. 4:
'. . . te [Constantine] divina praecepta, illum [sc. Maxentium] superstitiosa
maleficia [sequebantur].' How completely this pagan interpretation adver-
tises the official view is well shown by a comparison with the passage in
Eusebius, *H.E.* ix. 9. 3: Μαξεντίου δῆτα μᾶλλον ταῖς κατὰ γοητείαν μηχαναῖς
ἢ τῇ τῶν ὑπηκόων ἐπιθαρσοῦντος εὐνοίᾳ, &c.

[2] *Incerti paneg. Constantino Aug. d.* 26. 1–2 (p. 309): 'summe rerum sator,
cuius tot nomina sunt, quot gentium linguas esse voluisti (quem enim ipse
dici velis, scire non possumus), sive in te quaedam vis mensque divina est,
qua toto infusa mundo omnibus miscearis elementis et sine ullo extrinsecus
accedente vigoris impulsu per te ipse movearis, sive aliqua supra omne
caelum potestas est, qua hoc opus tuum ex altiore naturae arce despicias. . . .'

[3] After what I have said in the text, I think that I can still maintain my
position undisturbed against H. Grégoire, *Byzantion*, xiv, 1939, 351.

pagan rhetorician, Nazarius,[1] still declares that heavenly hosts sent by God, *divinitus missi*, came to the aid of Constantine at the gates of Rome. By this ready invention of legend he tries to evade any mention of the revelation of the initials of the name of Christ. But even *he* admits that the power of the godhead, *vis divinitatis*, cast the enemy to destruction[2] and that the divine aid was a reward for the piety of the Emperor.[3] But he preserves a complete silence about the identity of the god, 'who assists you in all your undertakings, *divinitas obsecundare coeptis tuis solita.*'[4]

The same attitude on the part of the pagans is revealed in the inscription on the triumphal arch, set up in Rome in A.D. 315, according to which Constantine won his victory 'at the instigation and direction of god', *instinctu divinitatis*, and, although on the ornaments of the reliefs Sol appears, that pagan deity to whom Constantine was still bound by some few feeble ties, the inscription does not more closely define the heavenly power that lent the aid. The Senate was compelled to accept the confession of Christian faith by its Emperor.[5]

Of some of the enlightened Roman senators, with their leaning towards Neoplatonic belief in one supreme god, who may have played a part in the development of the attitude of the Senate, we have a little closer knowledge. Aradius Rufinus was, until the 27th of October A.D. 312, governor of Rome and, as from the 22nd of November, Constantine restored him to his position of trust. Ceionius Rufius Volusianus had been governor of Rome under Maxentius, a little before Aradius; Constantine again appointed him governor at the end of A.D. 313. Of these two personalities, Aradius Rufinus and Ceionius Rufius, who belonged to the senatorial aristocracy, we might say that they were 'pagans with a touch of Constantine' or, rather, 'of Milan'. Symmachus records that 'Aradius worshipped the gods without a trace of superstition, *simplex caelicolum cultus*, and dedicatory inscriptions still survive, which he made during his proconsulate of Africa to

---

[1] *Nazar. paneg.* 14. 1 (p. 167 Guil. Baehrens). See also A. Knöpfler, *Historisch-politische Blätter*, cxli, 1908, 195 f.

[2] Ibid. 27. 5 (p. 177).   [3] Ibid. 7. 4 (p. 162 f.).

[4] Ibid. 13. 5 (p. 167).   [5] See Note 25, p. 132.

the two fashionable deities of the age of Constantine, Sol and Luna. Ceionius Rufius bears on a Roman inscription the title "most religious", *religiosissimus*. His son devoted himself to the study of philosophy. For long years he was in the close confidence of Constantine—governor of Rome during the first war between Constantine and Licinius, December A.D. 313 to August 315, consul in A.D. 314, chief of a section of the Empire, *praefectus praetorio* in A.D. 321.'[1] There were other pagan notables, too, whom Constantine retained in his service, placing much reliance on their breadth of outlook and their experience. In Rome there was also the pressure of tradition on the Emperor; whilst, on the other hand, the persons concerned were helpless before the omnipotence of the Emperor and were bound to take things as they found them.

In A.D. 315 Constantine again visited Rome. Certainly, on this occasion of the ten years' celebration of his rule, he displayed no lesser pomp than the majority of his predecessors; in fact, the magnificence and brilliance that surrounded the sovereign only grew with the age of the monarchy and the weakness of the Empire. Constantine, too, assuredly regaled the 'plebs' with public games, imposing in their scale and overloaded with entertainments. All the deeper must have been the indignation aroused among the pagans of Rome, on the one hand, and the satisfaction of the Christian masses on the other, by the fact that Constantine, on the days when his *vota decennalia* were celebrated, when thanks were given for the ten years of rule just past and happiness implored for the decade to come, did not allow the performance of the traditional ceremonies.[2] To perform such ceremonies had always been accounted a patriotic duty, to refuse them a revolutionary act, and that was why the periodic vows had been main occasions for the persecutions of the Christians. It was still fresh in public memory how the dazzling celebrations of the twenty years' jubilee of Diocletian had been the prelude to the

[1] A. Piganiol, op. cit. 62 f.
[2] Euseb. *Vita Const.* i. 48; cf. 3. 15. At his subsequent *decennalia* Constantine kept on cancelling the traditional elements, as J. Geffcken, op. cit. 95, has observed. At his *vicennalia* Constantine was finally estranged from the Senate; see also below, and *J.R.S.* xxxvii, 1947, 10.

bloodiest persecution.[1] This, combined with other insults and blunders, may well have produced the tension that from now on can be observed between Emperor and Senate. The legendary biography of Pope Sylvester, writes Piganiol,[2] tells of the disapproval felt by the senators for Constantine's utterances. It seems that tokens of this hostility are actually to be observed. Constantine was obviously trying to soften a resentment of this kind when, on the 20th of August A.D. 315, he appointed Vettius Rufinus governor of Rome. He was a well-known personage of the age of Diocletian who had grown old in the administration of Italy and was a member of the great pagan priestly colleges—*pontifex Solis, Salius Palatinus,* and *augur*. But all this availed little, and it may have been just Constantine's anger at the resistance of the Senate that led him to infringe its legal privileges. On principle, no doubt, he was quite right. The great senatorial landowners, able to bribe the corrupt officials with their measureless wealth and to terrorize the provincials by means of their many agents, permitted themselves ever-increasing deeds of violence. They simply took possession of the land of the small men in their vicinity. Their sons dragged off the daughters of these poor folk, at their own sweet will, and the sufferers could get no real justice in court. Criminal cases of this kind were assigned to Roman judges, because the accused belonged to the Senate, and those judges, being themselves senators, got the accused out of their mess. It was such abuses that Constantine meant to obviate, but with as little success as his successors.[3]

[1] Cf. *Klio*, xxxi, 1938, 323 ff.; N. H. Baynes, *C.A.H.* xii, 1939, 667.

[2] A. Piganiol, op. cit. 115. On the legend of Sylvester, see Levisohn, *Miscellanea Ehrle*, 2, 1924, 159 ff. New facts of importance that help us to form an idea of Rufinus are supplied by E. Groag, *Die Reichsbeamten von Achaia in spätröm. Zeit*, Diss. Pann. i. 14, 1946, 16 ff., according to which he was *consul ordinarius* in the years A.D. 316 and 323; his full name is C. Vettius Cossinius Rufinus.

[3] *Cod. Theod.* ix. 1. 1: 'Quicumque clarissimae dignitatis virginem rapuerit vel fines aliquos invaserit vel in aliqua culpa seu crimine fuerit deprehensus, statim intra provinciam, in qua facinus perpetravit, publicis legibus subiugetur neque super eius nomine ad scientiam nostram referatur nec fori praescribtione utatur. Omnem enim honorem reatus excludit, cum criminalis causa et non civilis res vel pecuniaria moveatur.' For the dating see: O. Seeck, *Regesten*, 165.

The utmost that he could achieve by such threats of criminal justice was to frighten the great lords a little. He ventured next on a much more fundamental measure against them. In a year earlier than A.D. 321 he is found endeavouring to change the character of the senatorial class in accordance with his own wishes. For if, as Nazarius attests,[1] he filled up the Senate with the flower of the municipal citizenship, this can only mean that he hoped by aid of rich Christian elements from the provinces to break up the solid block of the Senate and so crush their resistance. The attempt was probably bound to fail for economic reasons, even if the *Prosopographia* does prove the appearance of some new families. The great old noble families that had survived the awful crisis of the third century crowded out the new members, crushed their spirit, or moulded them to think with them. Thus it is that we still find in later days the same names in the influential circles of the Senate as under Constantine.

Our Emperor, however, after his *decennalia* spent little time in Italy and preferred to reside north of the Alps, in Sirmium or else, by choice, in Serdica. His favourite little joke about Serdica being his 'own Rome'[2] may have had its point. Such an aversion to Italy, the motherland, may be partly explained by Constantine's growing resentment of the stiff-necked pagans of Rome.

A later pagan writer, who hates Constantine and whose report betrays obvious chronological errors, maintains that he long continued to consult the *haruspices*.[3] He was, indeed,

---

[1] *Nazar. paneg.* 35. 2: 'ex omnibus provinciis optimates viros curiae tuae pigneraveris, ut senatus dignitas non nomine quam re esset inlustrior, cum ex totius orbis flore constaret.' Unless I am mistaken the significance of this quotation has till now escaped the notice of scholars.

[2] *Anon. cont. Dionis*, frg. 15, 1 (*F.H.G.* iv. 199): Ὅτι ὁ Κωνσταντῖνος ἐβουλεύσατο πρῶτον ἐν Σαρδικῇ μεταγαγεῖν τὰ δημόσια· φιλῶν τε τὴν πόλιν ἐκείνην συνεχῶς ἔλεγεν· "Ἡ ἐμὴ Ῥώμη Σαρδική ἐστιν."

[3] Zosim. ii. 29. 1 and 4: ἐχρῆτο δὲ ἔτι καὶ τοῖς πατρίοις ἱεροῖς, οὐ τιμῆς ἕνεκα μᾶλλον ἢ χρείας· ᾗ καὶ μάντεσιν ἐπείθετο, πεπειραμένος ὡς ἀληθῆ προεῖπον ἐπὶ πᾶσι τοῖς κατωρθωμένοις αὐτῷ . . . καὶ ἀφεμένου μὲν τῶν πατρίων . . . τῆς ἀσεβείας τὴν ἀρχὴν ἐποιήσατο τὴν μαντικὴν ἔχειν ἐν ὑποψίᾳ . . . καὶ . . . πρὸς τὸ ταῦτα καταλύειν ἐτράπη. See also the facts collected by Th. Preger, *Hermes*, xxxvi, 1901, 339 f.

superstitious, and it is quite possible that, even in the years after A.D. 314, he made use of the terrifying art of the *haruspices* and of the augurs, the watchers of birds. Even at the foundation of Constantinople he consulted the pagan prophets, for them to reveal to him the conditions needed to bring good luck to the act of foundation. But the practice became increasingly disagreeable to him as his relation to the Church became closer. Thus it came about that, some time in A.D. 318, he forbade the sacrifices of the *haruspices* in private houses, bound up as they were with all manner of conjurations and magic.[1] This edict probably became a dead letter, but there survives the text of laws which partly reassert, partly modify the prohibition.[2] The Senate may well have protested against it. The quite unusual journey of the governor of Rome, Septimius Bassus, to the Court in the summer of A.D. 318[3] was obviously undertaken to regulate some very tricky matter—and this prohibition was actually in force at the time. Bassus probably failed to induce the Emperor to give way, but the ebb and flow of negotiations in the sequel is very instructive for us. Constantine, to define his own position and to reassure the pagans, issued several fresh edicts which made it as clear as daylight how he treated the State cults of Rome and their defenders in this period.

It is probable that the common citizens, as well as the notables, had been troubled by the restrictions on the recourse to the *haruspices*. For the imperial ordinance dated 15 May A.D. 319,[4] which served to supplement the first edict on the subject, is addressed to the people of Rome.[5] It again forbids

[1] For a full discussion, see V. Schultze, *Zeitschr. f. Kirchengesch.* viii, 1886, 517 ff.   [2] See Note 26, p. 133.

[3] *Chronogr.* a. 354, ad a. 318 (*Mon. Germ. Hist., auct. ant.* ix, p. 67).

[4] For the dating see O. Seeck, *Regesten*, 58. 17, and ibid. 68. 29; 168. 170. Piganiol, op. cit., takes another view, inclining to transfer all these laws to the year A.D. 318. From our standpoint, the arguments of Seeck, op. cit. 58, deserve attention: 'If more than eight months fall between the date of the edict and its publication, the explanation lies in the contents. As the Edict was directed against the *haruspices*, it may well have run up against opposition from the pagan aristocracy of Rome. We may suppose, then, that the prefect of the City, who was regularly chosen from those circles, seriously delayed the publication out of personal hesitations and his need to consult the Emperor.'

[5] *Cod. Theod.* ix. 16. 2, 'ad populum (*sc.* urbis Romae!)'. The note of

the *haruspices* to practise in private houses their magic rites, which are branded as socially dangerous and which were certainly often malicious in purpose. But, to allay alarm, Constantine adds the further solemn explanation: 'But you, who believe that these practices are of value to you, may still visit the altars and shrines erected in public places and may still perform your solemn rites in the traditional manner.' Yet the Emperor cannot refrain from giving vent to his anger in the following scornful words. 'For we do not hinder you from practising in public the religious obligations inherited from the reign of the lost usurper (i.e. Maxentius).'[1] Constantine, in fact, openly insults paganism in Rome face to face. For in defending the art of the *haruspices* the pagans of Rome were also defending the belief in the activity of their own gods, even as Nicomachus Flavianus was still doing in A.D. 394. The Emperor, however, mitigates the severity of his proscriptions against the *haruspices* by solemnly guaranteeing the freedom of all other heathen religious practices. It was only seven years after the victory won in the name of Christ, and the battle now is not for the freedom of the Christian cult, but of the pagan—and that in Rome itself.

Contemporary with this edict is another, which likewise employs a contemptuous phrase for the pagan religion; it calls the business of the *haruspices* 'superstition', *superstitio*.[2] The priest who is an *haruspex* must not even cross the threshold of a strange house. The Emperor punishes their magic rites, if performed on the commission of a private person, by the cruel punishment of burning alive, while the instigators or clients suffer confiscation of property or banishment. Yet soon—early in A.D. 320—Constantine was compelled, no doubt under pressure of the population of Rome and, in particular,

mockery that refers to the usurpation of Maxentius proves that only Rome can here be in question.

[1] *Cod. Theod.* ix. 16. 2: '. . . Qui vero id vobis existimatis conducere, adite aras publicas adque delubra et consuetudinis vestrae celebrate sollemnia: nec enim prohibemus praeteritae usurpationis officia libera luce tractari.' Cf. the ordinance of the same date in *Cod. Theod.* ix. 16. 1: 'superstitioni enim suae servire cupientes poterunt publice ritum proprium exercere.'

[2] *Cod. Theod.* ix. 16. 1. On the date see Seeck, *Regesten*, 57. The scorching irony of the remark has already been emphasized by V. Schultze, op. cit. 520.

the Senate, to make a concession to the majesty of the Eternal City. He limits his threats against the practicians of conjuration and magic, *magicae artes*, to those who aim at the life of a fellow being or kindle the passion of love in the breasts of virtuous girls. On the contrary, he permits such magic as has a good object, such as curing the sick or protecting country-folk against cloudburst and hail; for 'such activity endangers no one's life or honour, but assures that God's gift, the harvest, and man's weary labours on it shall not be lost'.[1] This edict is completed by a new law of December A.D. 320,[2] which betrays the fact that tempers in Rome were still inflamed and needed to be appeased. Again, it is expressly emphasized that the official exercise of the activities of the *haruspices* in its connexion with the State religion is allowed, and, for example, supposing lightning to strike a public building, the result of the investigation by the *haruspices* is, in accordance with former practice, to be laid before the Court, with due notice of the evil that the sign portends. To lend greater emphasis, Constantine makes a great point of showing his approval of a recent announcement of the governor of Rome to similar purpose. The one and only thing forbidden is the conspiracy of the *haruspices* with private persons to do harm to others.

Throughout all this give and take Constantine is behaving like a good rider, now tightening, now slackening rein. One small but very significant event will show us how he combined energy with concession in dealing with the citizens of Rome. About A.D. 320 both the mints of north Italy and the Danube provinces used, in connexion with the same reverse type, the peculiar variation of the monogram of Christ with a small globe replacing the upper part of the P. Their regularity shows that they were acting on instructions from the central authority; but it is also certainly no mere chance that this type was not struck in Rome; there the advertisement of the Christian emblem of the Emperor is omitted.[3]

---

[1] *Cod. Theod.* ix. 16. 3. For the date, see Seeck, *Regesten*, 168. 170.
[2] See Note 27, p. 133.
[3] See my comments in *J.R.S.* xxii, 1932, 15, note 1 and *Pisciculi*, 3, note 8. Cf. H. v. Schoenebeck, op. cit. 39.

The reason why we can realize so clearly how the Senate made a national grievance out of the repulse of the *haruspices* and exaggerated it into a violation of the *mos maiorum* is because the same friction recurred fifty years later, and both parties again used the same arguments. There is also an event in the reign of Valentinian that may throw light on the beginnings of the pagan reaction. Under Valentinian, the Senate made a political grievance out of the restrictions placed on venerable Greek cults, on the occasion of the prohibition of sacrifices by night. We may infer, then, that this was not the first case, but that the Senate, from the time of the first Christian Emperor, had been carefully guarding the grand traditions of Greece. When we find Constantine, about this time, A.D. 319, entrusting the government of the province of Achaea—of Greece, that is to say—to a senator of comparatively high rank,[1] it was probably not the influence of Neoplatonic philosophers at court[2] or the Emperor's general benevolence to culture that decided him, but the pressure of the upper circles in Rome and the need to spare their sacred rites. Perhaps, it was even a gesture to show the imperial favour towards them.

The opposition to Constantine's endeavours to promote Christianity was not only expressed in the reaction that we have been following, breaking out, as it did, quite sporadically. We find a steadily stiffening resistance in Rome, which absolutely preserves its due loyalty, but still raises its voice against the new world. But, as such reaction had only very slender resources to oppose the imperial absolutism, and could only appear under disguised forms, art and literature were promoted to the front rank as its means of expression. Thus there arose a strange movement—we should call it to-day a battle of culture. It aimed at making the civilization and spirit of antiquity popular, by ostentatiously returning to the old gods, by representing the beauties of myth, and by promoting the values of ancient culture that were apparently so innocent politically—and, with all this, organizing opposition and working on the undecided. This political reaction, masquerading as

[1] E. Groag, *Die Reichsbeamten von Achaia in spätröm. Zeit*, Diss. Pann. i. 14, 1946, 21 f.　　　　　　　[2] So Groag, op. cit. 22.

a cultural movement, grew during its life of a century into something of real importance in world history. Directly or indirectly, we owe to it the chance of survival into our own times of the precious treasures of ancient civilization.

One peculiar expression of this propaganda may be seen in the issue of coins of a special kind, with pagan types, and limited to Rome.[1] It was an old custom that the men of rank, who arranged the popular amusements on the occasion of the great imperial vows of January the 3rd, should strike imperial coins adorned with types relating to the sea-festival of Isis Pharia that was celebrated at the beginning of the year, and should scatter them among the people. Clinging to this custom, the city prefects sprung from senatorial circles and their subordinates continued after A.D. 312 to strike these little bronze pieces at the New Year, with the types of Isis, Serapis, and Anubis, and so continued, not only under Constantine, but for some fifty years more.[2] The ingenious idea that gave rise to this propagandist coinage developed out of the strained atmosphere of the years following the fateful battle of the Mulvian Bridge. The old aristocracy, jibbing against the Emperor, confronts his pro-Christian policy with its own religion of mystery and romance. There is the same intention behind the trick of placing the mystical name of the Eternal City in the form of a cryptogram on the coins of Rome.[3]

It is, of course, to be understood that there were many more such ways and means which we can no longer check for Roman paganism to prove that *malgré tout* it was still alive.

It was in this age that the custom arose for the members of the senatorial order to erect surprising numbers of votive monuments with inscriptions to the old gods—a custom hitherto met with only here and there.[4] There is no ready way

[1] A. Alföldi, *A Festival of Isis in Rome under the Christian Emperors of the Fourth Century*, Diss. Pann. ii. 7, 1937. [2] Ibid. 12 and Pl. 1.

[3] H. Dressel, *Zeitschr. f. Numismatik*, xxii, 1899, 32 ff.; J. Maurice, *Numismatique Const.* i, 1908, 224 ff.; D. Lathoud, *Échos d'Orient*, xxiv, 1925, 180 f.

[4] We must not forget, however, that a rekindling of national Roman religious sentiment in these circles about the middle of the third century has already been observed by A. D. Nock in *Harvard Theological Review*, xxiii, 1930, 251 ff.

to separate these ostentatious dedications from the earlier and more commonplace variety. It is, in fact, very hard to determine the exact beginning of these boastful demonstrations in favour of polytheism. But there is no doubt that the movement was connected with Constantine's attack on the ancient pieties and that it grew continuously in power during the succeeding decades. For example, Caesonius Nicomachus Anicius Faustus Paulinus, as urban praetor, in September A.D. 321 erected a monument to Hercules near the *ara maxima,* in pursuit of this custom. In fostering the old religious tradition he was deliberately setting himself against the will of the Emperor. We must judge on similar lines the case in A.D. 319, when the priestly college of the *quindecimviri sacris faciendis* took personal part in the ceremony of the *taurobolium* in a famous shrine on the Vatican Hill.[1] The inscriptions that record the event indicate that the aristocracy was already displaying a provocative enthusiasm for such matters.[2]

This systematic defiance rose to the pitch of active opposition. Long after Constantine we can still observe how the senatorial dignitaries in their defence of polytheism simply refuse to be aware of the Emperor's anti-pagan tendencies. Only very late, at the end of the fourth century, was it possible to frighten them off these delaying tactics. This line of action probably began as early as the end of A.D. 312. It is in no small measure due to this passive resistance that the traditions of Rome in religion were able to survive under the great innovator, and that it was only much later that the Emperors ventured to make a serious attack on them.

[1] *C.I.L.* vi. 1. 135 = Dessau, *I.L.S.* 3409; *C.I.L.* vi. 508 = Dess. 4146.
[2] A trace of this challenging attitude may be seen in the popular astrological work (*Mathes.* iii. 5. 33) of Firmicus Maternus, who was of senatorial rank: 'In nono loco Sol ab horoscopo constitutus fabricatores deorum facit vel cultores divinorum simulacrorum vel ornatores deorum vel fabricatores templorum aut hymnologos et qui laudes deorum cum iactantiae ostentatione decantent, ex quibus rebus gloriam et honores habebunt.' Most of this he may have got out of his sources, but the *iactantiae ostentatio* probably truly reflects the new attitude.

VI

THE RELIGIOUS POLICY OF CONSTANTINE FROM THE BEGINNING OF THE PERIOD OF TENSION WITH LICINIUS TO THE DEDICATION OF CONSTANTINOPLE

FROM about A.D. 320 Constantine adopted an increasingly sharp attitude towards the pagans and leant more heavily than ever on the Church. The explanation usually given for his conduct is true to the facts. When the necessity for a settlement with Licinius began to be foreshadowed, the Christians in the East, who represented a considerable force, looked to Constantine for the improvement of their lot,[1] as against Licinius, who based himself on the opposite pole of paganism. It was as champion of the Faith that Constantine set about freeing them. But the way that this idea ran its course shows that there was no sudden change here, that the harsher policy was only an acceleration of the slower and more lenient policy of earlier years, as we have observed it from the autumn of A.D. 312.

Through the whole of the *De mortibus persecutorum* runs like a scarlet thread the thought that the bad Emperors persecuted the Church while the good ones protected it.[2] It was a one-sided idea, but obvious from the point of view of the Church confronting the world. The ancient Roman liberty was defended by the good, constitutional Emperor; the word 'liberty' now receives from Lactantius a new meaning—after how many others who shall say?—it is now 'religious freedom'.[3] The first citizen, who rises by merit to be leader of the Roman State, the *princeps* of Cicero's dream, later incarnated in

[1] Cf., for example, A. Piganiol, op. cit. 133 f.

[2] Lactant. *De mort. pers.* 4. 1 (on Decius): 'Quis enim iustitiam nisi malus persequatur'; or 3. 4: 'secutisque temporibus, quibus multi ac boni principes Romani imperii clavum regimenque tenuerunt, nullos inimicorum impetus passa (est ecclesia)', &c.

[3] Ibid. 5. 2 on Valerianus: 'Hic captus a Persis non modo imperium . . . sed etiam libertatem, quam ceteris ademerat, perdidit, vixitque in servitute turpissime.'

Augustus, is, for Lactantius, the Defender of the Christian Faith, whilst his opponents on the pagan side are violent rulers—tyrants. As *principes* in this sense Lactantius lauds Constantine and Licinius.[1]

At the same time Constantine represents his own victory over Maxentius in the same light to the eyes of the world. The agreement between Eusebius and the pagan rhetoricians, who report that Maxentius rested his defence on superstition and magic, *superstitiosa maleficia*, while Constantine was led by the divine will, *divina praecepta*, can only go back to an official court version; otherwise the pagans would never have branded their own religion as the spiritual possession of a defeated tyrant.[2] The inscription on the statue of Constantine in Rome, with the ensign of Christ in his hand, gives us to understand that 'in this sign of salvation I have restored to Rome, her senate and her people, their ancient liberty and glory, delivering them from the lawless yoke of the tyrant'.[3] Constantine is actually—though not in so many words—linking himself, as lawful *princeps*, to Christ; the inference can be drawn at once; the tyrant succumbed because he based his rule on paganism.

In the Edict of A.D. 319 against the *haruspices*, already quoted,[4] Constantine defines paganism in set terms as a 'perquisite of the bygone usurpation'—that is to say, of the régime of Maxentius. The Republican conception of the tyrant now received a Christian stamp, along with the revolutionary reinterpretation of the idea of *princeps*. It was no new thing, then, though it is often made out to have been, that in A.D. 324 Constantine took the field against Licinius as champion of Christ. The only point that is new is that Constantine emphasizes more than before that he is the executor of the true will of God against the persecutor[5] and that it is only as such that he

[1] Ibid. 1. 3: 'Excitavit enim deus principes, qui tyrannorum nefaria et cruenta imperia resciderunt.'

[2] The passages in ancient literature are quoted on p. 71, n. 1.

[3] From the text of Eusebius, *H.E.* ix. 9. 10, we might, with a slight deviation from the translation of Rufinus, reconstruct the original formulation thus: 'Hoc salutari signo . . . senatui populoque Romano et urbi Romae iugo tyrannicae dominationis ereptae pristinam libertatem splendoremque reddidi.'

[4] *Cod. Theod.* ix. 16. 2, quoted on p. 77, n. 1.

[5] Euseb. *Vita Const.* 2. 28–9; 3. 12; cf. ibid. 2. 24, 42; 3. 20.

is undertaking the battle to deliver the oppressed Christians —[1] a proper task for a genuine *princeps*. The masses of Christians, in their vastly increased numbers, now turn to him:

'For the Almighty requites the wicked, who in other parts of the world rage against the righteous, with a penalty for their sins that is only the heavier because it is delayed. For, though he is the most kind Father of the good, he is the severest judge of the godless. If it is my purpose to protect His religion, His holy worship, to whom can I turn better, whom better invoke to help me than That One, who has restored to the majority of mankind the rule of truth and wisdom.'[2]

After the ensign with the Christian monogram had helped Constantine to unite the Roman world under his rule and the effect of the ideas that we have been describing had been enhanced by success, the whole story was trumpeted even more loudly abroad. The mint of the new Christian capital is soon found celebrating the conquest of Licinius by a new reverse, with the legend, 'the Hope of all', *Spes publica*, and the type of the imperial standard with the emblem of Christ piercing with its point the snake of paganism.[3] In his own writings Constantine takes a delight in repeating the same mental picture;[4] and later he let himself be portrayed with his sons on a painting at the entrance to his palace in Constantinople, thrusting down to the pit of hell, in the shape of a snaky dragon, that hostile and destructive monster, that, by the agency of the

---

[1] Euseb. *Vita Const.* 2. 2–3.
[2] Lactant. *Divin. instit.* i. 1. 15 f.: 'nam malis qui adhuc adversus iustos in aliis terrarum partibus saeviunt quanto serius tanto vehementius idem omnipotens mercedem sceleris exsolvet, quia ut est erga pios indulgentissimus pater sic adversus impios severissimus iudex. cuius religionem cultumque divinum cupiens defendere quem potius appellem, quem adloquar nisi eum, per quem rebus humanis iustitia et sapientia restituta est?' For the dating see A. Piganiol, *Revue d'histoire et de philosophie religieuses*, 1932, 366 ff., with the literature.
[3] J. Maurice, *Num. Const.* ii, 1911, 506 f.; H. v. Schoenebeck, op. cit. 60 f. This type was certainly intended for issue in mass, like the other types of the new coinage. If, despite this, we have few specimens remaining, this, no doubt, proves that the issue was suddenly suspended. The reason for this measure will probably have been the movements of the aristocracy, to quiet which Constantine exerted himself greatly in A.D. 326.
[4] See Note 28, p. 134.

godless tyrants, tormented the Church of God; for the prophets of the Lord represented that monster as a snake with coils.[1]

We need hardly stop to recount how Constantine at this time raised the Church to the top of his edifice of State; the fact is established and its importance has already been duly made clear. We need only observe that it is now no general proclamation that secures the Church its new position of honour, but an uninterrupted sequence of special ordinances in its favour, which, like small tiles, compose a platform. The edicts tread one on the heels of the other. In A.D. 321 emancipation of slaves in church is declared valid. The Church is empowered to receive legacies. Private litigation may, at the wish of the two parties, be decided before a Church court.[2] But even more important from our point of view is the slow but steady gain of ground in a practice that hit the old ruling class very hard—the practice of Constantine, after his conquest of the East in A.D. 324, of choosing the great majority of his Eastern governors from the ranks of the Christians, the new converts, while forbidding such as were still pagans to perform the old official sacrifices. The same directions were given to the highest civil dignitaries, probably in the West as well.[3] But the administration of the West could not be transferred overnight to Christian hands, like that of the domains of Licinius, where Constantine could drive out Licinius' pagan followers and replace them by Christians whom he judged reliable. The heathen officials of the West had taken his side, in A.D. 306 in the West of Europe, in A.D. 312 in Italy and North Africa; thus Constantine found his hands tied both by his own earlier policy of toleration and by the loyalty of the officials.

The complete abolition of the pagan rites at the periodic vows of the Emperor assuredly made a deep impression even in the West. As early as A.D. 323 the Emperor had forbidden, under pain of severe punishment, any compulsion of men to the performance of pagan sacrifices on such anniversaries. One

---

[1] Euseb. *Vita Const.* 3. 3.
[2] For the last ordinance see *Cod. Theod.* i. 27. 2, and, on it, as against the view of Seeck (*Gesch. d. Unterg.* ii². 182 f.) consult A. Piganiol, *L'Empereur Constantin*, 1932, 138 f.; for earlier ordinances see above.
[3] Euseb. *Vita Const.* 2. 44; Sozom. i. 8. 5.

such enactment has come down to us which was publicly announced in Rome; it is very possible that it was directed only against abuses on the part of the leading circles in Rome.[1] In A.D. 325 the Emperor celebrated the twentieth anniversary of his reign, his *vicennalia*, in a Christian setting, in the presence of the bishops assembled for the Council of Nicaea. On this occasion the necessary panegyric was composed and delivered by a bishop.[2] At the same time appeared the portraits of Constantine with face turned heavenward, earnestly praying to the Christian Lord of the world.[3] What must have been the feelings of the pagans when they saw the Emperor paying every attention to the bishops,[4] whilst the Senate, to which even the hostile soldier-emperors had paid every reverence, could no longer count on imperial favour! At the opening of the Council of Nicaea Constantine would not take his seat until he was expressly requested to do so; following the strict etiquette of the age, he ranked the Church higher than himself.[5] When he kissed the empty eye-sockets of Paphnutius, the martyr was not only receiving the official recognition of his martyrdom, but also a distinction reserved for the very highest dignitaries and the members of the imperial family.[6]

Constantine enveloped the debates of the council with all the brilliance of a court. He conducted them in person, let the members come in at the public expense, entertained them in his palace. In all these respects the leaders of the Christian world took the place of the old aristocracy and, with even more privilege than they, formed the new entourage of the throne.

The Emperor, we know, took upon himself the task of making the unity of the Faith a reality, he allowed the resolutions of

---

[1] *Cod. Theod.* xvi. 2. 5, addressed to the *vicarius urbis*; see O. Seeck, *Regesten*, 62, 98, 173. The pagan creed is there called *superstitio* and the *catholica secta* is set up against it as the *sanctissima lex*. This contrast by itself reveals that the branding of *superstitio* is not restricted, as has been supposed, to magic.

[2] Euseb. *Vita Const.* I. I.

[3] Cf. for example, J. Maurice, *Num. Const.* ii, 1911, p. lxx f., and also my arguments in '25. Jahre Römisch-Germanische Kommission', 1929, 42 ff.

[4] Euseb. *Vita Const.* 3. 9, 10, 16, &c.

[5] A. Alföldi, *Mitt. d. D. Arch. Inst., Röm. Abt.* xlix, 1934, 42 f.

[6] Ibid. 41.

the council to be drafted by his chancellery, and let the official organs of State control their execution. In the course of these exertions he lost his way in the maze of theological subtleties and thus got Church and State politics irretrievably entangled. That the result of all this was to bring the organization of the Church within his unifying reform of the State has already been realized. The vital point for us to notice is that Constantine did not now for the first time attain the insight that it was absolutely necessary for that reform of the Empire that the age demanded, that the Church should be fitted into the machinery of the State. Plans of this kind had been maturing in his mind, but the realization of them had to wait for the moment when he found himself in sole possession of rule.

As a result of this, the attitude of the Head of the State naturally changed towards the pagans too, but not all of a sudden. An important symptom is the final disappearance of the old gods from the coinage about A.D. 320.[1]

Even before the breach with Licinius, in all the mints of Constantine, wreaths and surrounding legends announcing the periodic imperial vows were used on all the reverses of the small bronze pieces instead of the types of the pagan gods, and, most curiously, to the exclusion of all other ornament. It was certainly not without political intention that this was done. These new types, which express the personal feeling of loyalty and devotion to the lord of the Empire, and which could not, therefore, be objected to from the standpoint of Roman conservatives, are nothing but an adroit way of masking the banishment of the last of the Olympians from the coin-types.

The effort to oust paganism, however, was hampered for the time by the same fact which actually gave to that campaign a new impulse—by nothing more nor less than the defeat of Licinius in A.D. 324. In the Eastern provinces the oppressed Christians had before all else to be restored to their rights; the exalted principles of toleration of the Edict of Milan were still fresh in all men's minds, and that was a sufficient reason why the oppression of the one party could not be immediately succeeded by the oppression of the other.

[1] Cf., for example, H. v. Schoenebeck, op. cit. 39, 48, 58.

Immediately after his victory Constantine issued an Edict for the East, guaranteeing the free exercise of the old religions.[1] This edict is a most peculiar document, but one which faithfully reflects the changing moods of its imperial author. Constantine, in it, does not scruple to abuse his predecessors; he reproaches his subjects, who had tolerated the persecutions, with being even more evil than the barbarians, and he furiously denounces the belief in many gods as deception and confusion. Then again, he turns with complete submission to the Almighty, loses the legalistic style of the chancellery, and directs to God his fervent prayer and thanks, waxes enthusiastic over the grandeur of the divine order of the world, addresses himself in warm terms to the followers of the one and only true Christian Faith, and ends with the expression of his wish, his earnest wish that 'the erring and deceived' may be converted. But all this is merely the broad, baroque frame for an order of quite a few lines. 'The erring shall win the same peace, the same rest as the believers. Those who sunder themselves from the company of the faithful may still retain the sacred places of their false doctrines, if they so please.'[2] But it is no longer Christianity that is the tolerated religion, it is paganism. Nothing could better show the immensity of the revolution accomplished in the twelve years that had elapsed since the victory of the Mulvian Bridge. The spirit of the Milan Edict of toleration has now to be used, not to appease the adversaries of the Christians but the Christians themselves.

'What each man out of conviction undertakes himself, he shall not try to force on another. What a man sees and realizes for himself, let him serve his neighbour therewith, if he may; but if he avails not so to do, let him leave it alone. For it is one thing to undertake of one's own free will the battle for the hereafter, another to compel men by punishment to do so. I have stated this and explained it more fully than my grace intended [*clementia nostra* will have been the words of the Latin

---

[1] Euseb. *Vita Const.* 2. 47 ff. For the correct interpretation, see N. H. Baynes, Raleigh Lecture (1930), 19, and A. Piganiol, op. cit. 147 f.

[2] Euseb. *Vita Const.* 2. 56 (p. 64 Heikel): ὁμοίαν τοῖς πιστεύουσιν οἱ πλανώμενοι χαίροντες λαμβανέτωσαν εἰρήνης τε καὶ ἡσυχίας ἀπόλαυσιν. . . . οἱ δ' ἑαυτοὺς ἀφέλκοντες ἐχόντων βουλόμενοι τὰ τῆς ψευδολογίας τεμένη.

text] as I would not conceal my Christian faith. I have done so because, I am told, some men are saying that the usages of the pagan temples have been abolished together with the powers of pagan darkness. Indeed, I would so counsel every man, were it not that the rebellious might of false doctrines, to the injury of the salvation of us all, has struck its roots so terribly deep.'[1]

These words help us to realize how very strong the aggressive spirit of the Christians already was. But Constantine only remained faithful to this proclamation for as short a time as he had kept to the former programme of toleration in the opposite direction.

We have one or two more edicts of Constantine which hit the old religions hard, not exactly dated, but all soon after A.D. 324. At this time he forbids the erection of statues to himself and the religious worship of such statues in the pagan temples,[2] and in so doing he undermines the most essential political function of paganism, the worship of the Emperor. The same purpose was served when he forbade the participation of State officials at the rites of pagan sacrifice and when he abolished the pagan ceremonies at the recurrent festivals of the vows, &c. In the same period falls[3] his interference with the traditional religious ceremonies of the army—a measure which has not yet, as I think, been estimated in its true importance. The unconverted soldiers, from now on, must pray every Sunday to the Almighty. What really matters here is not the text of the prayer, which expresses a deliberately colourless conception of the divine nature, but the fact that the petition for the Emperor's welfare was not accompanied by pagan rites but was a prayer and nothing more. This is what the Christians had done from the first, in defiance of the State, until finally Galerius, with the most extreme reluctance, permitted it. But here there is no longer any question of Christians, but of that citadel of paganism, the army, which would have been only too glad to sacrifice. We must not forget that Licinius in A.D. 314 was still demanding sacrifice from his troops as a test of

---

[1] See Note 29, p. 134.

[2] Euseb. *Vita Const.* 4. 16 (p. 123 H.), Socrat. *H.E.* 1. 18.

[3] Euseb. *Vita Const.* 4. 19–20. As he connects this with the hallowing of the Sunday, the ordinance must logically belong to the same date.

loyalty.[1] But it is not certain whether Constantine ventured to carry this measure through. In the last resort the soldiers might perform a sacrifice to accompany the prayer. Apparently the Emperor also issued an edict against the trickeries of soothsayers after his victory over Licinius.[2]

[1] Euseb. *H.E.* x. 8. 10; cf. id. *Vita Const.* 1. 54; 2. 33.
[2] V. Schultze, *Zeitschr. f. Kirchengesch.* viii, 1886, 517 ff.

VII

CONSTANTINE'S LAST CONTACTS AND FRICTIONS WITH ROME BEFORE THE DEDICATION OF THE NEW CAPITAL

HOWEVER oppressive may have been the effects of the Emperor's religious policy in Rome, he continued to treat the Eternal City with consideration and respect. In A.D. 321 the mint of Aquileia, selected for that purpose by the Court, struck for the occasion of the Emperor's fifteenth jubilee silver coins on which the Senate, the 'plebs', and the city herself, are, as at the zenith of their glory, named at the head of the Roman world.[1] The bureaucracy of the time was completely centralized and, in the case of such special issues, the initiative of any subordinate officials is quite out of the question. These documents, original, authentic, of official character, must reflect the policy of the Court.

At the same time a panegyric, composed at the official instance of the Court, undertakes to act as a mouthpiece for the demand of Rome that she shall again become the permanent residence of the Emperor.

'There is only one thing needed to perfect the happiness of Rome— a great thing, but the only one—to see her deliverer, Constantine, and his blessed sons, the Caesars, that she may enjoy, to the full measure of her longing, the delight of welcoming you; and that, if the interest of the State demands that you must leave her, she shall only send you away with the assurance of winning you again.'[2]

The consuls of A.D. 322 were members of the noblest senatorial aristocracy. One of them was actually a member of the family of the Anicii, which was only to make the transit to Christianity much later in the future. Maximus Basilius, also

[1] See Note 30, p. 134.
[2] *Nazar. paneg.* 38. 6: 'Unum modo est quo fieri possit Roma felicior, maximum quidem, sed tamen solum, ut Constantinum conservatorem suum, ut beatissimos Caesares videat, ut fruendi copiam pro desiderii modo capiat, ut vos alacris excipiat, et, cum rei publicae ratio digredi fecerit, receptura dimittat.'

an aristocrat, was governor of Rome for four years from
A.D. 319 to 323. The last edict of Constantine known to us,
before he began operations against Licinius, relates to the
supply of Rome with bacon.[1] At the same time Constantine
appointed his half-brother Dalmatius praetor, not merely to
encourage the senators to undertake the office of praetor, with
its heavy burdens,[2] but also to flatter Rome. A noble Roman
poet, Publilius Optatianus Porphyrius, immediately before the
conquest of the East, is still praising Rome as the centre of the
world, in fact as being even then restored to her true position
as head.[3]

But the religious friction with the senatorial circles had not
yet ceased. At the end of A.D. 325 the Emperor sent an order
to the deputy of the prefect, the *vicarius urbis*, forbidding that
Christians should be compelled, on the occasion of the festivals
of the imperial vows, to offer sacrifice after the old rites,[4] a
measure directed against abuses on the part of high dignitaries, it may be. And immediately after the battle of Chrysopolis, on the 18th of September A.D. 324, the rebuilding of the
old Byzantium on the shores of the Bosphorus began, now re-
christened Constantinople and destined to be the new capital.[5]

To understand how Constantine came to think of building
his new city and what he meant by it we must stop for a
moment to consider the gradual estrangement of his predecessors from Rome. Later, in another context, we shall see
how the third century robbed Rome and Italy of their privileges, ousted the senators from the high military commands,
replaced the praetorian garrison, on which Rome's political
aspirations could be based, by troops from the Danube, whose

[1] A. Piganiol, op. cit. 141 f.
[2] *Cod. Theod.* xii. 17. 1 (19 Jan. 324) and W. Ensslin, *Rhein. Mus.* N.F.
lxxviii. 209 ff.
[3] *Optat. Porph.* carm. 11. 1 ff.: 'Fortia facta ducis toto dominantia iam
nunc orbe canam, quis laeta suo sub principe tanto rursum Roma tenet,
mundi caput, inclyta, culmen.'
[4] *Cod. Theod.* xvi. 2. 5; O. Seeck, *Regesten*, 62. 35, and 173.
[5] See my remarks in *Numizmatikai Közlöny*, xli, 1942, 3 ff. (= *J.R.S.*
xxxvii, 1947) where all the literature is quoted; on the ceremonies attending
foundations, and on the inaugural festival of *consecratio*, and the closing
festival of *dedicatio*: D. Lathoud, *Échos d'Orient*, xxiii, 1924, 289 ff.

minds were filled not with the prerogatives of Rome but with the interests of the Empire, and finally disbanded the old guard altogether. And we shall see how, in spite of all, the age, while stripping the city of all real power, left undiminished the glory of Rome's ancient fame.

Now we need only make one point. The wars that raged without ceasing from the thirties of the third century to its end had raised the military duties of the Emperor to an importance high above any others. His residence must now be fixed at a place suitable to be his army headquarters. What suited his requirements best were such junctions of communications or strategic bases as Cologne on the Rhine front and, behind it, Treves and Lyons; Sirmium (Mitrovitza in Slavonia) in the district of the Danube frontier, and, behind it, Thessalonica and Serdica (modern Sofia); then, in north Italy, back from the Danube front, Milan; in the East, Antioch behind the Euphrates—not to mention other, more occasional head-quarters. All these cities were gradually developed up to the point when the Emperor, with his whole Court and his body-guard, could at any moment resort to them.

Another point to be mentioned in passing is that Rome did not submit in silence to the continuous attacks on her leading position. In A.D. 238 the city had destroyed Maximin when he was on his way to attack her, and had thereby given the army such a lesson of its power that, though it never succeeded in recovering its lost position, every new Emperor, with his armies, would for fifty years take every risk, even that of exposing the frontiers, in order to dash to Italy and make his obeisance before the majesty of the capital. Though this practice ceased with Carus, yet something of the old payment of honour survived. The splendid festivals of the imperial *quinquennalia* and *decennalia* were held in the ancient resi-dence; they were not only festivals at which thanks were given for the blessings of the recent past and prayers offered for a happy future, but included a triumphal procession, cele-brating all victories in war before the Senate and people of Rome. Rome, then, remained as before the ideal centre.

This conception of Rome was not even affected when Dio-cletian, seeking a central position where he could communicate with his colleagues round him, chose and developed Nicomedia as his residence, thus being determined in choice of site not by military considerations but by the needs of administration and the lines of communications. But this, as we shall see later, gave rise to some rivalry with Rome, and the idea of a new Rome was born. Even in earlier times every provincial city wanted to be like Rome. But now it was no question of the idle dreams of petty provincials, but of the deliberate purpose of the supreme ruler.

The founder of the Tetrarchy, in founding Nicomedia, was assuredly led by higher considerations than his predecessors, who had erected their imperial headquarters behind the fronts. Their city buildings, of which we have just spoken, were one and all designed to serve military tactics. But even in a soldier's eyes Nicomedia was something different—a strategic, not a tactical, base, suited in every way to perform the function of a heart in the circulation of the blood of the Empire. It cannot, therefore, be disputed that the government through the whole course of the third century was looking for a centre fit to answer the ever-growing demands on it. Constantine, then, as we shall soon see, only marked the end of a long development.

The creation of these new residences, of which we have been speaking, led to building activity on the grand scale. The earlier of them—Sirmium, Treves, Milan, for example—only with the slow lapse of years attained the status of imperial cities; the later ones—such as Thessalonica, Serdica, and the rest—were converted at a stroke, by the magic utterance of the imperial will, from provincial cities into magnificent residences. The building of them, therefore, demanded an extraordinary expenditure of force.

Lactantius is very anxious to suggest that this building fever was a mere whim of Diocletian.

'To all this was added a special, uncontrollable passion to build, and this involved an equally drastic oppression of the provinces, which had to supply workmen, artisans, vehicles and all the requirements of building. In one place rose Courts of Justice, in another a circus, here a mint, there an arms factory, here a palace for his wife, there another for his daughter. All of a sudden, a large section of a city would be torn down. Everybody must emigrate with wife and children, just as if the city had been conquered by the enemy. And, when it was all done and the provinces had been ruined, up rose the cry: "Back! It won't do. It must all be done again." So mad was Diocletian in his career, while he aimed at making Nicomedia as great as Rome.'[1]

But this was certainly no mere individual madness. After the shattering effects of the world crisis, amid the general misery of the age, a few dozen great landowners had acquired mammoth fortunes. So, too, the imperial building was accelerated in an unexampled degree, in contrast to the building of municipalities and private citizens, which perished in the financial chaos.

In the soul of every free citizen of antiquity slumbered the dream of becoming the hero-founder of a city. Thus it was that the soldiers who reached the throne, in the untrammelled exercise of their power, developed a grand activity in building that has an overwhelming effect on us even to-day. The excavations of Salonica[2] (first suggested by the present author together with H. von Schoenebeck and carried through with splendid success by E. Dyggve) have revealed a vast complex of buildings, almost two-thirds of a mile in length. They include not only the imperial palace, but a great domed temple, a square triumphal arch, mighty arcades and halls, and a great hippodrome—all brought into being by the Emperor Galerius, on the unified plan of one great architect. The palace quarter of Galerius in Serdica cannot have been much less extensive; and, no doubt, the palace buildings in Sirmium, begun by Marcus Aurelius and carried forward by the Illyrian Emperors, need fear no comparison with those of Salonica. The amazing proportions of the imperial architecture in Treves are familiar to all, as also is the grand palace and fortress of Diocletian, built after his abdication, in Spalato, which stands to this day. The age displayed its creative powers, not in the withering arts of painting and sculpture, but in architecture,[3] and in this field

[1] See Note 31, p. 134.
[2] E. Dyggve, *Laureae Aquincenses*, ii, Diss. Pann. ii. 11, 1942, 63 ff.
[3] G. Rodenwaldt, *C.A.H.* xii, 1939, 561 ff.; id, *Forsch. u. Fortschr.* xv, 1939, 245; A. Boëthius, 'Roman Architecture from its Classicistic to its Late Imperial Phase' (*Göteborgs Högskolas Årsskrift*, xlvii, 1941, 8).

it was no longer private initiative but the boundless power of the absolute monarch that found its artistic expression.

Constantine had got to know the great buildings of Diocletian and Galerius in the East inside and out with his own eyes. He had been at home from childhood in the splendid palaces of the Roman West; as Emperor he had made use of them, one after the other. Neither his ambition nor his power was less than that of any of his predecessors. How could he fail, then, to form the ambition of accomplishing what they had done?[1] But, in all his activities, his ideas kept changing, until at last his designs reached their end; and so, too, his plans for a new city residence did not at once reach finality.

Constantine had long carried plans of the kind in his head. When he first thought of building his new Rome in Serdica (the modern Sofia) on the extreme border of his domains, at the gate of the East, he was certainly already counting on gaining possession of the East.[2] Beside this site in the interior, perhaps in place of it, he may also have had thoughts of Thessalonica, that vital junction of land and sea routes which had already undergone its transformation into an imperial residence.[3] Byzantine sources profess to have information that Constantine, after the conquest of Licinius, began at first to raise the walls of his new residence on the site or in the vicinity of ancient Troy. But it is not hard to prove that this is a mere invention, drawn from a tendentious local tradition. Ilium, the legendary predecessor of Rome, was to be claimed for Constantinople, which was, therefore, to appear more illustrious and permanent than the Eternal City.[4]

---

[1] F. Lot, *La Fin du monde antique*, 1927, 40 f., is of the opinion that the foundation of Constantinople is 'not the goal of a process of evolution. If it is true that Rome had ceased in A.D. 284 to be the capital, if men's minds had become accustomed to dissociate from Rome the habitual residence of the Emperor, it was force of circumstances, not any premeditated plan, that was to blame.' But what does 'evolution' mean except that which is fulfilled in course of time 'by force of circumstances' without there having been any 'premeditated design'?

[2] Anon. Cont. Dionis., frg. 15, 1 (*F.H.G.* iv. 199); cf. Zonar. xiii. 1 (3, p. 13 Büttner–Wobst); see also L. Bréhier, *Rev. hist.* cxix, 1915, 244 f.

[3] Kedren, p. 495, 22 ff. Bonn.

[4] A. Alföldi, *Num. Közl.* xli, 1942, 4 ff. = *J.R.S.* xxxvii, 1947, 10 f.

These early moves were enough in themselves to betray the Emperor's intention of getting away from the West. After the battle of Chrysopolis, when he was no longer thrown back, as he had been for so long, on the material and moral forces of the West, he made his decision like a flash of lightning. He realized that Byzantium enjoyed far greater natural advantages than Diocletian's majestically rebuilt Nicomedia.[1] But it was no mere chance[2] that he sought the site of his city in the neighbourhood of the centre of administration and traffic chosen by Diocletian, on the border of two seas and two continents; and, perhaps, it was not just chance again that he did not make precisely the same choice as his hated predecessor. He borrowed his ideas and developed them, here as almost everywhere else, in his own modifying style.

It is obvious that, once Constantine had set the Church deep in his structure of Empire, there was no longer a place in the State in its new Christian organization for the old capital with its kernel of paganism. That meant that, as Rome failed to become Christian, there was an entirely new role waiting for the new capital. The Emperor's agents began to sweep in from all sides the gold and silver treasures of the old gods to finance the rebuilding of the new capital[3] and adorn it with the theft of famous statues; the treasures of Delphi[4] and other shrines made their way to the Bosphorus. Even in Rome people must have begun to feel that the twilight of the gods had begun. Only a little before the murder of Crispus a Christian court-poet applies to Constantinople the expression, 'the other Rome', *altera Roma*,[5] but tones it down by the remark that it

---

[1] See Note 32, p. 135.

[2] See also O. Seeck, *Gesch. d. Unt.* i⁴. 71; E. Kornemann, *Die römische Kaiserzeit*, in Gercke-Norden, *Einl.* iii³, 2, 1933, 115 and 139 ff.; L. Bréhier, *Rev. hist.* cxix, 1915, 268 ff. Further literature may be found in E. Gerland, Byzantinisch-neugriech. Jahrbücher, x, 1934, 104 f., and E. Gren, *Kleinasien und der Ostbalkan*, 1941, 156 ff.

[3] Liban. *Or.* 30. 6 (3, p. 90 F.).

[4] E. Homolle, *Bull. Corr. Hell.* xx, 1896, 729.

[5] Optat. Porphyrius, *carm.* 4. 1 ff.: 'Imperii fastus geminant vicennia signa | pagina flexuoso tramite vota notat. | Constantinigenis Helicon det talia natis | munera, devotis haustibus ora rigans. | hos rupes Cirraea sonet videatque coruscos | Ponti nobilitas, altera Roma, duces. | sed nunc te, victor,

is, as he imagines, the sons of Constantine who will have their thrones there; the Emperor himself will stay in the old Rome.

It is astonishing that in spite of all this the majestic traditions of the Eternal City had not lost their power to move the passionate reformer. Eusebius writes,[1] immediately after the East had fallen into the hands of Constantine, that Licinius, when he ventured to abolish the wise and ancient laws of the Romans, introduced in their place savage and barbarous legal principles of his own. What does Eusebius mean by this? Is he defending the policy of Constantine and justifying the attack on Licinius in terms of the old senatorial tradition?[2] Or better, are we to see again in A.D. 324, as once in A.D. 312, the familiar picture of the *princeps*, who restores Roman freedom and destroys the tyrant, who is branded as a barbarian? The idea was certainly common form. Lactantius, for example, scoffs at Licinius as a barbarian, in his *De mortibus persecutorum*. Or perhaps there is no need to see the Emperor behind the expression. Was it the compelling power of a literary convention that for once entrapped the eloquent bishop, born enemy of the 'traditions of the fathers', the *mos maiorum*, though he was? In any case it is possible that the form of words employed gives us the authoritative style of Court propaganda; for Constantine was just then making one more attempt to come to terms with the guardians of the Roman tradition. If we may assume this, we can explain why Constantine, in spite of his adoption of the intolerant attitude of the Church, still allowed the title of chief priest of paganism, *pontifex maximus*, to remain among his ranks.[3] It was a concession that did not concern paganism as a whole, but only the aristocracy of Rome, which alone was interested in the matter. The Roman notables may also have found a little comfort in

vicennia picta honorent.' The glorification of Crispus, *c.* 5. 30 ff., compels us to date it before his murder, and *carmen* 4 is only the introduction to 5; this verse, then, must belong to a date just before the visit of Constantine to Rome; but it was already written under the sign of the twenty years' jubilee.

[1] Euseb. *H.E.* x. 8. 12 f. (p. 896. 10–24 Schwartz).

[2] R. Laqueur, *Eusebius als Kirchenhistoriker seiner Zeit*, 1929, 195 ff.; id. *Probleme der Spätantike*, 1930, 8 f.

[3] A. Bernareggi, *Scuola cattolica*, anno 41, ser. 5, vol. ii, 1913, 237 ff., dealt with this problem exhaustively in detail.

the fact that the Emperor was then showing surprising favour to a group of educated men of refined religious views, the Hellenic Neoplatonists. In A.D. 326, for example, Nicagoras, the priest of the Eleusinian mysteries, *daduchos*, made a journey to Egypt, that home of magical wisdom, by the vehicles of the imperial post—obviously with the authority and support of the Emperor;[1] and Constantine maintained friendly relations both with the theosophist Hermogenes and with Sopater, until at a later date the latter was put to death by the Emperor or by his Christian confidant, Ablabius.[2]

In A.D. 324 after the defeat of Licinius, as in A.D. 312 after the Italian campaign, an occasion seems to have arisen for Constantine to employ the Senate as the tool of his policy. In A.D. 312 he had let the Senate vote to him the title of 'first Augustus'. So now he caused the Senate to arrange for the murder of Licinius at his hands in order to shunt on to it the odium of his death.[3] Constantine's final attempt to find some sort of compromise with the senatorial circles of Rome is represented by his resolve to celebrate his *vicennalia* together with the *decennalia* of his sons in A.D. 326 in Rome, and display there all the glories of his recent victories. He had already, a year before, held one celebration of the *vicennalia* in a Christian setting in the East.

His journey was heralded by some crafty pieces of propaganda, which we may reasonably regard as an olive branch held out in the direction of the Capitol. From the beginning of A.D. 326 gold coins were struck in honour of the Emperor and his sons for the approaching jubilee, praising the 'eternal glory of the Senate and people of Rome' and even representing a model senator, in dress embroidered with gold and with the globe and sceptre, the attributes of world rule, in his hands.[4] This implies the most complete obeisance of the Emperor

---

[1] J. Baillet, *Comptes-rendus de l'Académie des Inscriptions et Belles-Lettres*, 1922, 282 ff.; P. Graindor, *Byzantion*, iii, 1926, 209 ff.; O. Schissel v. Fleschenberg, *Klio*, xxi, 1927, 361 ff.

[2] O. Seeck, *RE*. iiiA, 1006 f.; A. Piganiol, op. cit. 159 f.

[3] Zonar. 13. 1 (3, p. 175 Dind.).

[4] I have gone fully into this in *Num. Közl.* xli, 1942, 6 ff. = *J.R.S.* xxxvii, 1947.

before the Senate, such a gesture as his predecessors had long omitted to make. And, of course, it was not only the coins passing from hand to hand that celebrated the representatives of the ancient traditions of the city, but with them the whole apparatus of propaganda at the command of the Court, both in art and literature. We may quote in the same context the cross-word phrases that the imperial poet, Optatianus Porphyrius, weaves into his verses. They do not aim at any poetical effect but at artful surprise of the readers, while they sing of the overflowing delight of the *Quirites* at those blessings that the peace of the Emperor brings.[1]

At the same time it appears that the Roman knights were, as a special favour, reorganized. They were not fitted into that new framework of the society of the Empire that was passing into a caste system, but were restricted to Rome and, as a second order, inferior to the Senate, were equipped with privileges. Constantine, then, raised that stratum of the population that stood in wealth and standing above the mass of the 'plebs', without attaining the high level required for senators, to a new platform; among such were the members of the guilds of shippers, *navicularii*, for example.[2] This new knighthood of Rome is celebrated by the reverse type of the rider, *eques Romanus*, which was issued together with the *aeterna gloria senatus populique Romani* and the *senatus*.[3]

After this overture Constantine arrived in Rome. But, though he flattered the Eternal City with dazzling display and brilliant games, though he engaged in conversation with the magicians and the astrologers, he never lost sight of his Christian aims. He could not even conceive of reconciliation with the Senate on any other terms than its submission to his christianization of Rome.

Constantine now gave Rome her first Christian governor in the person of Acilius Severus,[4] who stood in very close relations with Lactantius, and who held the office from 4 January

---

[1] Optat. Porph. c. 16. 9 ff. Cf. the verses interwoven c. 19, and c. 10. 21 ff.

[2] See Note 33, p. 135.

[3] Full details in my paper in *Num. Közl.* op. cit. = *J.R.S.* xxxvii, 1947.

[4] H. v. Schoenebeck, op. cit. 73 ff.; A. Piganiol, op. cit. 171.

A.D. 325 to 12 November A.D. 326.[1] We are not at all surprised to hear that Constantine moved about a good deal in
the Christian circles of Rome.[2] But even more remarkable is
the fact that now for the first time, as it appears, he endowed
the Eternal City with a Church of Martyrs on a scale unpre-
cedented before, which became the model for important church
buildings of similar character in the Holy Land and other
places.[3] With this splendid building, worthy of the capital,
with its lavish revenues, with its amazing equipment of gold
and silver, was it not the intention of Constantine to set on
Rome, the ideal centre of the Empire, a Christian stamp?
That, in my opinion, was his aim.

But if it was so, the plan failed. Constantine fell out with
the pagans. We have the pagan account in Zosimus, following
Eunapius. According to this account, which for all its errors
and its malicious tone contains a kernel of historical truth,[4]
the troops who had accompanied the Emperor had to march,
on the occasion of a pagan festival in Rome, up to the Capitol
to perform the customary ceremonies. The Emperor meant to
attend the festival himself, to avoid wounding the feelings of
his soldiers. But when he set eyes on the procession, he could

[1] *Chronogr.* a. 354 = *Mon. Germ. Hist., auct. ant.* ix. p. 67.

[2] Of his social intercourse with a Christian jurist we happen to hear from
an inscription: Diehl, *Inscr. Christ. Lat. Vet.* 748.

[3] H. v. Schoenebeck, op. cit. 88 ff.; A. Piganiol, op. cit. 171; H. Lietzmann, *Petrus und Paulus in Rom*², 1927, 189 ff., E. Caspar, *Gesch. des Papsttums*, i, 1930, 124 f. W. Seston argues for A.D. 333 as the date of the actual
beginning of the building of the cathedral in an important paper (*Cahiers
archéologiques*, ii. 1947, 126 ff.). I wonder if complications about the destruction of tombs in the building area in 333 could not be eventually compatible
with an imperial resolution made in 326. In any case the occasion for planning such a grandiose church in Rome was much less far to seek in 326 than
at any other date after Constantine's final break with the old capital of the
Roman world.

[4] I agree in this point with L. Bréhier, *Rev. hist.* cxix, 1915, 241. But in
my conviction, it is plain that the error in the account, the story of the conversion of Constantine, is to be explained as Th. Keim has already explained it
in *Der Übertritt Constantins d. Gr. zum Christentum*, 1862, 52: 'The whole story
simply arose out of a combination of the declaration of the Emperor against
paganism in Rome in A.D. 326, the murder, at the same time, of Crispus and
Fausta, and the old tradition, found both in Celsus and Julian, of Christianity
as the great institution for the cleansing of all sins.'

not control a sudden spasm of fury, began to curse and swear, and, in thus making a final breach with tradition, drew on himself the hatred of the Senate and 'plebs'.[1] This was not the only explosion of anger of which we hear. The air must have been full of electric tension. In front of the Emperor marched, as ever in full view, the bodyguard, bearing the ensign with the emblem of Christ, when he went up to the temple of Jupiter Optimus Maximus. Three years earlier, when he forbade that Christians should be forced to make pagan sacrifices, he had called paganism a senseless superstition, *superstitio*, and the Church of Christ the most holy law, *sanctissima lex*.[2] Assuredly similar thoughts must now have flashed through his mind. His fury may have been increased by the memory of the purely Christian jubilee, held the year before in Nicomedia, and by the fact that he was not accustomed to being unable to carry out his will. But Zosimus may be right in saying that his whole soul was in a turmoil, as he had only quite recently ordered the murders of his wife and eldest son.[3] But his army was pagan in sentiment. An official report of the 1st of March A.D. 326 survives, according to which his men greeted him as he entered the camp with the cry: 'Our revered lord, Constantine Augustus, may the gods preserve you; your salvation is our salvation too!'[4] That was why Constantine did not wish to affront his troops by abstaining from their ceremonies when he came to Rome. But his tortured nerves got beyond his control.

Zosimus adds that everybody—all the pagans, that is to say

[1] Zosim. ii. 29. 5: τῆς δὲ πατρίου καταλαβούσης ἑορτῆς, καθ' ἣν ἀνάγκη τὸ στρατόπεδον ἦν εἰς τὸ Καπιτώλιον ἀνιέναι καὶ τὰ νενομισμένα πληροῦν, δεδιὼς τοὺς στρατιώτας ὁ Κωνσταντῖνος ἐκοινώνησε τῆς ἑορτῆς. ἐπιπέμψαντος δὲ αὐτῷ φάσμα τοῦ Αἰγυπτίου (abusive term for Ossius) τὴν εἰς τὸ Καπιτώλιον ἄνοδον ὀνειδίζον ἀνέδην, τῆς ἱερᾶς ἀγιστείας ἀποστατήσας, εἰς μῖσος τὴν γερουσίαν καὶ τὸν δῆμον ἀνέστησεν. Cf. the objections, raised by Philostorgios, which J. Bidez brought to light (*Byzantion*, x, 1935, 413 f.), calling attention to the fact that a trace of it is also to be found in Julian's work, the 'Caesars'.

[2] *Cod. Theod.* xvi. 2. 5.

[3] Zosim. ii. 29. 2–3.

[4] *Cod. Theod.* vii. 20. 2: 'Idem A[ugustus] cum introisset principia et salutatus esset a praefectis et tribunis et viris eminentissimis, adclamatum est: Auguste Constantine, dii te nobis servent: vestra salus nostra salus. . . .' Cf. O. Seeck, *Regesten*, 106 and 176.

—cursed Constantine for this act, and that was why he sought out a rival to Rome, to which he could transfer his residence.[1] Constantinople, we have seen, had already received her new name, the building was already well advanced; but it *does* look as if Constantine, in founding her, had originally designed a more modest part for her. The rebuilding seems to have begun inside the old circuit of walls.[2] According to the evidence of respectable authorities,[3] it was not until A.D. 328 that Constantine greatly extended the range of the city-walls, after choosing an auspicious day, on the advice of his astrologers.[4] If this is correct, it was in that year that Constantine, exasperated by the obstinacy of Rome, decided not to leave the ideal centre of the Empire in Rome, but to found an anti-Rome, which should become the city of Christ.

Several years passed, and the new capital was still not ready. Constantine could not take up residence there, could not yet realize his intentions. If we may suppose that he had not yet begun to entice senators to Constantinople, little may yet have been known in Rome of his revolutionary plans. Moreover, Rome now received, as if in token of appeasement, a new pagan governor in the person of Anicius Julianus, A.D. 326 to 329.[5] Here is another fact of importance. The personification of the new anti-Rome, which, as we shall see, represents Constantinople as rival to Rome, does not appear on the coins until

---

[1] Zosim. ii. 30. 1: Οὐκ ἐνεγκὼν δὲ τὰς παρὰ πάντων ὡς εἰπεῖν βλασφημίας πόλιν ἀντίρροπον τῆς ʻΡώμης ἐζήτει, καθ᾽ ἣν αὐτὸν ἔδει βασίλεια καταστήσασθαι. Leo Gramm., p. 84, 19: δεδιὼς δὲ τὴν σύγκλητον ʻΡώμης διὰ τὸ εἰς Χρίστον πιστεῦσαι, ἐξῆλθε δῆθεν ἐπὶ τὸν τῶν Σκυθῶν πόλεμον. This statement is accepted by Th. Keim, op. cit. 55, for example.

[2] Seen in this light by Th. Preger, *Hermes*, xxxvi, 1901, 342.

[3] *Chron. Pasch.* a. 328, p. 527 f. Bonn; Patria Constantinopoleos 55 f. (*Script. orig. Cp.* p. 142 f. Preger).

[4] So Th. Preger, op. cit. According to O. Seeck, *Regesten*, 69 and 178, however, Constantine on the day in question was residing in the West. It might, however, be possible that the date is correct as far as the year is concerned and only wrong in its fixing of the day, as we know that on 1 March A.D. 328 Constantine was still in Nicomedia and might therefore have resided several times at the beginning of the year in the city that he had already begun to build. According to the scanty dates that we possess he had been present in Constantinople before, on 11 June A.D. 327; we find him in Heraclea on 3 August and 25 October, A.D. 329.   [5] O. Seeck, *RE.* i, 2199.

A.D. 330. The issues of Constantinople and of the other mints with her continue to proclaim in solitary grandeur the fame of the goddess Roma—at such a moment a highly significant fact.[1] The anti-Rome was not yet proclaimed.

About A.D. 330 the first signs of the great change begin to appear. The Empress-mother Helena, who had died early in the year, was buried in Rome[2] in the porphyry sarcophagus which, by the military character of its reliefs, betrays that it was primarily intended for a man—in fact, for the son of Helena.[3] Constantine, then, only left to the city of Rome the empty shell of his mother in the mausoleum which he had originally had made for himself,[4] when after the battle of the Mulvian Bridge he had still no thought of making a new centre of authority and religion for his Empire in place of Rome.

[1] Cf. my remarks in *Num. Közl.* xli, 1942, 5 = *J.R.S.* xxxvii, 1947.

[2] Cf. F. W. Deichmann, *Arch. Anz.* 1941, 735 ff. The death of Helena is placed by O. Seeck, *RE.* vii, 2822, between 335 and 337, in error. I return to this point later.

[3] P. Franchi de' Cavalieri, *Mélanges d'arch. et d'hist.* xxxvi, 1916/7, 246 f. (giving the older literature) ; J. Ebersolt, *Byz. Zeitschrift,* xxx, 1930, 586 ff. ; H. v. Schoenebeck, op. cit. 89, note 1 ; E. Caspar, op. cit. 125.

[4] See also F. W. Deichmann, *Arch. Anz.,* 1941, 740.

VIII

RELIGIOUS INTOLERANCE GETS THE UPPER HAND IN THE POLICY OF CONSTANTINE

In the closing years of Constantine the power of the Church grew and spread without ceasing. In place of toleration of paganism came its suppression.[1] The Neoplatonist Sopatros, who was still employed in A.D. 330 in ascertaining that mystical conjunction of the heavenly bodies that promised happiness and permanence for the new capital to be dedicated, fell in one way or another a victim to this intolerance.[2] The Emperor loudly proclaims his favour for the Christians,[3] presses on the populations of the cities the abandonment of their old cults, and actually rewards them for it.[4] Only in one point does he still find it necessary to apply the brake—when it comes to the imperial cult and when a complete uprooting of the customs at the festivals might have impaired the loyalty of his subjects. This is clearly to be seen in a famous Umbrian inscription. The town of Hispellum asked that it might hold the festival and games of the imperial cult in Umbria in place of the Etruscan Volsinii; until then the two provinces had celebrated them together. It further asks for permission to erect a temple for the adoration of the dynasty. As a reward for this loyalty the Emperor bestows on the town the name of 'Flavia Constans'—a quite unusual distinction as coming from

[1] L. Salvatorelli, *Ricerche religiose*, iv, 1928, 322 ff.

[2] According to Suidas, s. v. 'Sopatros' (4, p. 407, Adler), Constantine had him put to death to prove that he was no longer pagan in his sympathies; according to Zosimus, ii. 40. 3, it was Ablabius who did this, a Christian and Constantine's right-hand man; according to Eunapius, *Vit. soph.* 462. 2 ff., it was superstitious courtiers who brought Sopatros to his death. See also O. Seeck, *RE.* iiiA, 1006 f.

[3] *C.I.L.* iii. 7000 = Dess. 6091. Constantine writes that the petition of the inhabitants of Orcistus in Phrygia is supported by the fact that 'quibus omnibus quasi quidam cumulus accedit, quod omnes ibidem sectatores sanctissimae religionis habitare dicantur'.

[4] Cf. the inscription just quoted and the comments of Th. Mommsen, *Gesammelte Schriften*, 8, 24 ff. See further Euseb. *Vita Const.* 4. 37-9; Sozom. ii. 5. 7-8; Theophan., p. 38 de Boor.

him. It is all to no purpose that he reviles the cults of polytheism as 'deceit of infectious superstition', *contagiosae super-
stitionis fraudes*: for he allows a temple to be set up to the
gens Flavia, to its imperial members alive and dead, and allows
a special priest to be appointed for it, the *pontifex gentis
Flaviae*.[1] Constantine goes on to grant the grace that gladia-
torial games—so bitterly condemned by the Church—shall be
held there at the customary anniversaries of the imperial
festivals. All is subject to the condition that the cult shall not
be defiled by any pagan rite.[2] This solution had the desired
effect of satisfying both parties. But if we regard it dis-
passionately, it is a case of changing the name without changing the fact. Temple and priest belong only to divine beings.
Moreover, the popular festivals that were permitted, the procession of the images of the old gods in the parade of the *pompa
circensis* and the bloody combats, still, even without any
sacrifices, preserved for these anniversaries of the *gens Flavia*
a certain pagan character. And this is but one link that we
happen to be able to feel in the chain of policy that Constantine pursued in regard to the imperial cult; even to the end of
his days he tried to retain it in this 'disinfected' form. In
what was, perhaps, his last edict he freed priests, past and
present, of the imperial cult in the provinces from heavy public
burdens.[3] His attitude remained a model for his successors,
and even Christians enjoyed dignities in the 'sterilized' cult of
the Emperors.[4]

Religious practices, we see, when entangled with the senti-
ments of loyalty, could not just be abolished. Constantine
therefore only stripped them of such features as were absolutely objectionable. The Roman aristocrats, of course, did
not fail to observe this sore spot in Constantine's anti-pagan
policy, and in this way they succeeded in the following decades

[1] *C.I.L.* xi. 5283 = Dess. 6623; Mommsen, op. cit. 42 f.

[2] *C.I.L.* xi. 5265 = Dess. 705; cf. Mommsen, op. cit.; E. Kornemann,
'Beiträge zur alten Geschichte', *Klio*, i, 1901, 138; A. Piganiol, *Revue des
Études anciennes*, 1929, 139 f.; de Domenicis, *Historia*, iv, 1929, 270.

[3] *Cod. Theod.* xii. 5. 2. Earlier favours granted in A.D. 335, *Cod. Theod.*
xii. 1. 21. See also Mommsen, op. cit. 33.

[4] V. Schultze, *Zeitschr. f. Kirchengesch.* vii. 369; P. Monceaux, *Histoire
littéraire de l'Afrique chrétienne*, iii, 1905, 47 ff.

the Religious Policy of Constantine 107

in rescuing a few festivals which had the character of popular entertainments and in preventing the destruction of a few temples.[1]

But it was not only the public interest that might have suffered from the complete suppression of the imperial cult. The morale of the State might have been shaken if the Emperor, placing himself on the side of the Christians, had attacked because of their pagan origin all the ideas connected with the greatness of Rome or the living actuality of Rome, the city. Constantine was still compelled to show indulgence in this point when he began his campaign of devastation against the old religions—a campaign that now rose in a single crescendo.

Such evidence as survives to-day gives the impression that in the lifetime of Constantine the devastations were limited to the East—and this impression probably corresponds to the facts. We must also be careful not to represent the destruction caused by Constantine as either greater or less than it actually was. On the one hand, the triumphant reports of churchmen about the complete destruction of paganism have been proved by the evidence of inscriptions to be grossly exaggerated.[2] The Christian priests generalized these devastations, if only to obtain justification from the practice of the first Christian Emperor for the complete blotting out of their adversaries after his death. The sons of the great reformer themselves sought to justify their own acts by his ordinances.[3] On the other side, the wounds inflicted on the cults of polytheism were exaggerated by embittered pagan historians.[4]

Paganism finally died of the wounds suffered in the last years of Constantine—but it was a case of 'delayed action'. The aggressive policy which found its full development in these years had begun many years earlier and had been slowly ripening. But still it implied a new and violent revolution

[1] A. Alföldi, *A Festival of Isis in Rome under the Christian Emperors of the Fourth Century*, Diss. Pann. ii. 7, 1937, 30 ff.
[2] J. Geffcken, op. cit. 96 and 280, and cf. V. Schultze, *Gesch. d. Untergangs d. griech.-röm. Heidentums*, i, 1887, 326, and ii, 1892, 219, 262 f., 315, 318 (who cites all the facts).
[3] *Cod. Theod.* xvi. 10. 2.   [4] J. Geffcken, op. cit. 95, note 41.

quite incompatible both with the toleration proclaimed to the Christians by the Edict of A.D. 312 and with that promised to the pagans in A.D. 324. No tears need be shed if a few oriental temples, in which immorality was rife, were destroyed. Many an Emperor before Constantine had laid his hands on temple treasures in his hour of financial need or had caused precious monuments of art to be hauled from Greek temples to beautify Rome: but none of them had intended, as Constantine intended, to destroy. Fundamentally this was a campaign of annihilation, like that of Diocletian a generation earlier against the Christians.

It was in these years A.D. 330 to 337 that the destruction of the seats of pagan cult began.[1] But we must not think of a sudden general attack like that of Diocletian, who, at the beginning of his persecutions, had all the Christian churches, everywhere and at once, destroyed. The work of devastation began now sporadically; the special measures needed were discussed and arranged case by case. In one place bronze doors were dragged away; in another the metal revetments of the temples were torn off at the Emperor's command. Elsewhere the gold and silver that covered the idols was stripped from the frames, while statues of bronze were melted down. Many masterpieces of art had already been carried off to beautify Constantinople.[2] From now on poverty was the rule in pagan shrines.[3] Some temples Constantine closed, but not all—as Eusebius and others maintain.[4] Out of these acts of plunder a huge capital was amassed which Constantine could employ—or waste—at his own sweet will, to build Constantinople, to reward his soldiers and favourites, or to increase his issues of the precious metals.[5]

Among the pagan shrines destroyed by Constantine were

[1] A. Piganiol, *L'Empereur Constantin*, 1932, 185 f. (giving the facts).

[2] Euseb. *Vita Const.* 3. 54 (pp. 101 ff. Heikel); Iulian. *Or.* 7, p. 296. 2 Hertlein.

[3] Liban. *Or.* 30. 6 (3, p. 90 Foerster); *Or.* 62. 8 (4, p. 350 Foerster).

[4] Euseb. *Vita Const.* 4. 23; Iulian. op. cit.; Eunap. *Vit. soph., Aedes.* p. 461 Boissonnade; *Chron. pasch.*, p. 561, 10 Bonn; Oros. vii. 28. 28; *Socrat. H.E.* i. 3; Sozom. *H.E.* ii. 5. 1 ff.

[5] The sources in A. Piganiol, op. cit. L. Wrzoł, *Weidenauer Studien*, i, 1906, 251 f.

some that hurt Christian piety by their presence on the scenes
of Holy Writ or aroused resentment by their immoral rites.[1]
In other cases his destructive purpose was directed against
particularly popular shrines in order to annihilate the demonic
powers ascribed to their idols. Such, for example, was the
destruction of the temple of Asclepius at Aegae in Cilicia.[2] It
cannot be excused by the plea that it was already in ruins and
required therefore to be pulled down.[3] Here and there single
shrines were still restored.[4] But the final settlement with
paganism was well on its way when Constantine for ever closed
his eyes.

But the contrast, on the other side, is all the more exciting.
The paganism of Rome still stands inviolate—and that although
the imperial edicts aimed at the temples, like all imperial
ordinances, were everywhere valid. It is not out of the question
that Constantine may have had time to issue a general prohibition of sacrifice before death baulked him in his task of
pulling up paganism by the roots.[5] This is reported by
Eusebius—and he stood so close to the events in question that,
even had he wished it, he dare not have made such an assertion
if its falsity was obvious to all his companions and contemporaries. Constantine's own son Constans too, four years
after his father's death, in A.D. 341 appeals back to such a
prohibition.[6] Even if Constans exaggerated the contents of the
prohibition, even if they were actually not so much formal
prescriptions as general threats against sacrifice, to frighten
the uncertain and accelerate the conversion of others,[7] the
importance in principle of the prohibition is not weakened
thereby.

[1] The facts are collected in V. Schultze, op. cit. 1. 51 ff.; J. Geffcken,
op. cit. 95.

[2] So K. Müller, *Kirchengeschichte*, i², 1929, 360; cf. Sozom. ii. 5. 5.

[3] As Geffcken, op. cit., n. 42, believes; but he misjudges Constantine when
he says of him that 'he never thought of laying a destructive hand on any
venerable temple or any ancient cult'.

[4] Dates in Geffcken, op. cit., note 44.

[5] See Note 34, p. 135.

[6] *Cod. Theod.* xvi. 10. 2.

[7] See Note 35, p. 136.

IX

THE OLD ROME AND THE NEW

On 17 May A.D. 330[1] at the solemn celebration of his twenty-five years of Empire the supreme ruler of the State dedicated his new capital and by so doing gave his Christian organization of the State a centre free from any touch of paganism.[2] This peculiarly Christian character of Constantinople, which the Church writers emphasize with a natural pride, has, indeed, been called in question by a scholar who knows his world of late Rome well.[3] But his plea is robbed of its force by the small bronze coins and medallions, issued in mass, on which on the sceptre of the 'Tyche', the goddess who personifies the city, is shown the globe set on the Cross of Christ—which means to say that the new capital is the ideal centre of the Christian world-empire.[4] On Constantine's own confession God appeared to him in a dream and ordered him to found the new residence.[5] Its dedication was accompanied by a solemn Mass.[6]

The names of outstanding personalities of history have often come to express the conception of rule. The 'Kaiser' is so called after Caesar; the modern Hungarians have coined their name for king, 'király', from the name of Charles the Great. Now the name of Rome, the conqueror of the world, meant simply 'ruling city'; this fact and all the ideas that were tied up with it could not just be wiped out of men's memories. Why, even

[1] Hesych. Πάτρια Κπόλεως 42 (*Scriptores orig. Cp.* I. 18 Preger); *Chron. pasch.* a. 330 (*Mon. Germ. hist. auct. ant.* ix. 233 f. Mommsen).

[2] Euseb. *Vita Const.* 3. 48 (p. 98 H.); Socr. *H.E.* I. 16; Sozom. *H.E.* 2. 3; Augustin. *De civitate Dei,* 5. 25; Oros. vii. 28. 27, &c.

[3] O. Seeck, *Geschichte d. Untergangs d. ant. Welt,* iii². 426 f.; similarly, L. Bréhier, *Rev. hist.* cxix, 1915, 255 ff., to whose paper I refer for details.

[4] I have proved this, quoting the evidence of the coins mentioned below in my paper in *Num. Közl.* xli, 1942, 9 = *J.R.S.* xxxvii, 1947. See also H. v. Schoenebeck, op. cit. 41 and 61 f.

[5] Sozom. 2. 3; *Cod. Theod.* xiii. 5. 7 and cf. O. Seeck, op. cit. i⁴. 473.

[6] Malalas, 13, p. 320. 18 Bonn and cf. V. Schultze, *Altchristl. Städte und Landschaften,* I, *Konstantinopel,* 1913, 7, note 2; 8, note 7; H. Lietzmann, *Sitzungsber. d. Preuss. Akad.* 1937, 268.

Constantine himself could not escape from this deep complex of thought, and it was a foregone conclusion that, when he made a new centre for the Empire in its new Christian form, that centre could only be a 'Rome'. So when the Emperor founded his new 'city of Constantine', in all respects spiritual and material he copied the old Rome, in order to replace it by the new.

A fresh and vivid light is thrown on these endeavours by that allegorical conception of Constantinople as a female figure which appears on the memorial coins issued for the festival of dedication in Rome. They are not exact copies of the 'Tyche', set up in the form of a statue in the new capital, as we see it, for example, on the splendid silver medallions of the mint of Constantinople;[1] but the use of a little poetic licence made it possible to emphasize even more fully the political significance of the guardian spirit. On these coins the bust of Constantinopolis regularly corresponds to a bust of the goddess Roma—it is obviously set in deliberate contrast to her or, to put it more plainly, it represents Constantinople, the 'city of Constantine', as the anti-Rome.[2]

This variety of the 'Tyche' is characterized by that heaping up of symbols that in the course of syncretism had become such a feature of the pagan religions. There is no question but that Sopatros or some other of those philosophers, mystics, and astrologers who had taken part in the preparations for the dedication of the new capital thought it out.[3] This mass of divine attributes aimed at representing Constantinople as Queen of Peace, of Victory, and of Plenty—like the real world-conqueror, Rome. The winged 'Tyche' who sets her foot on the prow of a ship, with the crown of towers and the cornucopiae, is a goddess who combines in herself the symbols of Rhea, Abundantia, Victoria, and Ceres, to whom as *Victoria Augusta* is ascribed the highest praise that Roman

---

[1] For all details and for the specialist literature see my paper quoted in n. 4, p. 110.

[2] Eutrop. x. 8. 1: 'primusque urbem nominis sui ad tantum fastigium evehere molitus est, ut Romae aemulam faceret.' For the details one may quote the paper of A. Bréhier, *Rev. hist.* cxix, 1915, 249 f.

[3] Th. Preger, *Hermes*, xxxvi, 1901, 338 f.

sovereignty admits—a just victory, and who is deliberately
shown beside the *dea Roma*. How characteristic it is of the age
that the first believer in Christ to sit on the throne of the
Caesars could only reach a close definition of the position of his
new Rome in face of the old in the pagan conceptions of late
Roman thought, in the pagan idiom! This same method of
casting reflections to and fro between the two capitals can be
traced farther in the spiritual shaping and the material realization of the new Rome.

One such example of assimilation of one to other is provided
in the establishment of a new Senate in Constantinople. One
can only ask in astonishment how Constantine, who completed
the creation of a monarchy that included everything, ever
came to create in his new residence the body that had been a
thorn in the flesh to most of his predecessors.[1] It was indeed
an amazing thing to do. It corresponded to no political reality;
it was simply derived by deduction, in full harmony with the
abstract spirit of the age. If there is to be a Rome, there must
be a Senate. For his new Senate Constantine not only had a
palace built in the finest residential quarter of his city, but he
tried to entice both wealthy provincials and noble families out
of the Eternal City—to give the new *curia* a more genuine
Roman touch. With this aim in view he erected splendid
houses for those few senatorial families—probably Christian
families, in the main—that followed his call.[2] But there is
something stranger still to come. The new Rome now being
forged on the anvil of the imperial autocracy must not only
have a Senate, but it cannot do without an artificial parallel to
those citizens of Rome who had once conquered the world;
a Roman people had to be got together in Constantinople. The
local coins issued in A.D. 335 celebrate this population of new
citizens under the venerable official title of *populus Romanus*[3]

---

[1] O. A. Ellissen, *Der Senat im oströmischen Reich*, 1886, 16 f.

[2] Zosim. ii. 31. 3; Sozom. *H.E.* ii. 3. 6; ii. 34. 4; Glycas 4. 462. Πάτρια
Κπολέως 40 (*Script. orig. Cp.* 1. 17 Preger); ibid. 1. 63 (2, p. 146 Pr.); 1. 67 (2, p.
148 Pr.); 70 (ibid. 149), &c.; O. A. Ellissen, op. cit. 10 and 12; Ch. Lécrivain,
Le Sénat romain depuis Dioclétien à Rome et à Constantinople, Bibl. des
Écoles Fr. d'Athènes et de Rome, fasc. 52, 1888, 217 ff.

[3] J. Maurice, *Numismatique Constantinienne*, i, p. cliii and ii, 1911, 536 f.

—perhaps on the occasion when the Emperor assured their prosperity by giving them freedom from taxation.[1] The 'plebs' of Rome itself might base on the incomparable deserts of its fathers its claim to be officially provided with bread and other necessaries of life; but the imperial favour after A.D. 332 gave the same great privilege, with all the burden it implied for the community, to the citizens of Constantinople, who had done absolutely nothing to deserve that high grace.[2] It all goes to show that, in the intention of the founder, the new residence was to have a Roman and a Latin character.[3] Here, as in the focus of the Christian Empire, Constantine celebrated on 15 July A.D. 335 the thirtieth jubilee of his reign.[4]

The new capital was to be a Rome from top to toe. Its founder delights in calling it 'the second Rome', δευτέρα 'Ρώμη, *altera Roma*,[5] and in releasing it from its original place in a province he makes it into a special district, to correspond to Rome, its model. This did not merely imply that the new capital became a new administrative district; it meant much more than that. Constantinople received a privilege which raised it in law to the level of Rome. I mean the *ius Italicum*, which Italy itself had by now lost and which was only enjoyed by the citizens of Rome. With it went the advantage that the landowners paid no land-tax and were also freed from the heavy burden of the new system of taxation, the *capitatio*.[6] Again, in fixing its extent, as in fixing the number of its inhabitants, Constantine aimed at making his new capital like the old.[7] Constantinople, like Rome, is the 'city of the seven

[1] *Cod. Theod.* xi. 16. 6. Cf. O. Seeck, *Regesten*, 41. 1, 89. 33 and 183.
[2] *Zosim.* ii. 32. 1; *Chron. Pasch.* a. 332 (p. 531 Bonn = *Chron. Min.* i, p. 234 Mommsen) and ibid., p. 533. 10 Bonn; Socrat. *H.E.* 1. 35; Philostorg. *H.E.* 2. 9 (p. 22 Bidez), &c. Other information, with the literature, in E. Gebhardt, *Studien über das Verpflegungswesen von Rom und Konstantinopel in der späteren Kaiserzeit.* Diss. Dorpat, 1881; L. Bréhier, *Rev. hist.* cxix, 1915, 253 f.
[3] E. Stein, *Geschichte des spätrömischen Reiches*, i, 1928, 197.
[4] O. Seeck, *Regesten*, 183.
[5] Cf. F. J. Dölger, *Zeitschr. f. Kirchengesch.* lvi, 1937, 1 ff. In *Cod. Theod.* xiii. 5. 7 the mention of the name Constantinople, *aeternum nomen*, may also be a challenge to Rome. See V. Schultze, *Altchristl. Städte und Landschaften*, I, *Konstantinopel*, 1913, 6, note 1; W. Ensslin, *Gnomon*, vii, 1931, 262.
[6] The facts in L. Bréhier, *Rev. hist.* cxix, 1915, 252.
[7] *Chron. Pasch.* p. 530, Bonn, &c.

hills'—one of them called 'Capitolium'—and, like Rome, it is divided into fourteen districts.[1] It possesses a new imperial palace, the chief feature of which is that it is not smaller than that of Rome.[2] Near the palace extends the Hippodrome, with the Emperor's box, just as in Rome[3]—there is a forum and buildings of State just as there.[4] The starting-point of the imperial network of roads, the *milliarium aureum* in the Roman forum, is copied in Constantinople by the 'million' in the Augustan square. Here too there were vast Christian basilicas, one of which, as the counterpart of the famous Altar of Peace of Augustus, was named 'Irene', the Church of the Holy Peace.[5] We have already seen how the 'Tyche' of the new city was a copy and a rival of the goddess Roma, and was to appropriate to herself the powers that Rome enjoyed of overcoming and blessing the world. This circumstance throws light on the fact that Constantine, following the proposal of Sopatros or some other theosophical adviser, was able to use the mystical pagan name of the old capital, 'Flora', in its translation into Greek, 'Anthusa', for his new capital.[6] To rival Rome on her high cultural level, the great innovator caused vast numbers of statues and other works of art to be carted into his new city.[7] And he must needs have his philo-

[1] V. Schultze, *Altchr. Städte*, &c., 1913, 8 and 177 f.; L. Bréhier, *Rev. hist.* cxix, 1915, 247, 254.   [2] Zosim. ii. 31. 1.

[3] *Chron. Pasch.* a. 328 (p. 528 Bonn). Cf. J. Ebersolt, *Le Grand-Palais impérial de Constantinople*, 1910, 13 f.

[4] Cf. J. Ebersolt, op. cit. 14 f.; V. Schultze, *Altchr. Städte*, &c., 1913, 7 ff., 175 ff.; A. Piganiol, op. cit. 202; D. Lathoud, *Échos d'Orient*, xxiii, 1924, 296 f.

[5] H. Lietzmann, *Geschichte der alten Kirche*, iii, 1938, 136; V. Schultze, *Altchr. Städte*, &c., 1913, 4.

[6] G. Wissowa, *RE.* i. 2393, gives the sources and literature. D. Lathoud vainly tries to deny the truth of this information, *Échos d'Orient*, xxiv, 1925, 181 ff. We have already seen that, of the secret names by Lydus, that of Eros was actually in use between A.D. 320 and 324. See p. 80, n. 3. Moreover, the whole idea fits perfectly into the frame that we have been sketching.

[7] See also Chr. G. Heyne, *Soc. Reg. Scient. Götting. Comm. Class. Hist. et Philol.* x, 1788–9, 80 ff.; xi, 1790–1, 1 ff.; xii, 1792–4, 273 ff. A large part of the later evidence may now be found in *Script. Orig. Cp.*, ed. Th. Preger, fasc. 1–2. See also V. Schultze, op. cit. 17 ff. and id., *Zeitschr. f. Kirchengesch.* vii, 1885, 352 ff.

sophers and rhetoricians, too. There, as founder of the new Christian Rome,[1] he arranges that he shall be buried, after he had, a short time before his death, been admitted to the Church as a simple believer,[2] and, when death drew nigh, received baptism, following the custom of the age, in order to be freed from his sins by the ceremony of baptism and so enter Paradise.[3]

All this makes it the more interesting that Constantine never for a moment dared question the priority of the true Rome over the new Rome, his capital. Simply by calling it 'second Rome',[4] he voluntarily subordinates his own creation to the true mother-city of the Empire. The case was really just as Julian, speaking in the presence of Constantius II, defined it: Constantinople is as much greater than any other city as it is less than Rome.[5] The title of the members of the new Senate is only *viri clari*, not *clarissimi*, as for the Roman senators.[6] The governor of the city did not, like the governor of Rome, receive the illustrious title of *praefectus urbi*, but only that of *proconsul*—an inferior and little-regarded rank. Such obeisance before the Eternal City actually enhanced its political power, despite the Emperor's turning away from it. For, when Constantine so exactly defined the rank of his new capital, the supremacy of old Rome was surely established. And we must not forget that the structure of Roman society on its way to complete mechanization was held together by a strict order of precedence and vitalized by the struggle to mount the social ladder. The leading ideas of Augustus had continued for centuries to be authoritative. So too now, all that Constantine

---

[1] A. Kaniuth, 'Die Beisetzung Konstantins des Grossen', *Breslauer Hist. Untersuch.* xviii, 1941.

[2] So K. Müller, *Kirchengeschichte*, i². 361. See also Ed. Schwartz, *Gött. gel. Nachr.* 1904, 545; id., *Kaiser Konstantin und die christliche Kirche²*, 1936, 63; F. J. Dölger, *Konstantin der Grosse und seine Zeit* 1913 (19 Suppl. der *Röm. Quart.*), 437 ff.; K. Müller, *Zeitschr. f. Neutest. Wiss.* xxiv, 1925, 285 f.; id., *Hist. Zeitschr.* cxl, 1929, 269 f.; F. Stähelin, *Zeitschr. f. Schweiz. Gesch.* xvii, 1937, 413.

[3] F. J. Dölger, op. cit. 429 ff.

[4] Id., *Zeitschr. f. Kirchengesch.* lvi, 1937, 18, note 31.

[5] Iuliani, *Or.* 1. 4 (p. 16 Bidez).

[6] The evidence in E. Stein, op. cit. i. 194, note 7. This reduction in rank may have been partly the reason why the noble Roman families did not think it worth their while to migrate to Constantinople.

cast long retained the impress of his individual will. And so it was here. Yet we have to recognize that the arrangements made by those who in moments of decision have to settle the fate of millions are only a step on the path of evolution, which does not even then come to a stop and which regularly refuses to advance in the direction planned. This was to be Constantine's fate in the new arrangements that he made in reference to Rome. But we have still to see what the real purpose of those arrangements was.

When Constantinople openly became the ideal centre of the Christian Empire, Rome, the old capital, renounced by the Emperor, was *ipso facto* bound to be left the citadel of the old traditions. The relation of the two cities to one another is well expressed by the busts on the coins above mentioned that personify *Urbs Roma* and *Constantinopolis*. On the shoulder of the personification of New Rome is shown the globe of the world, set on the Cross of Christ, symbolizing the new capital of Christendom. What then, we may ask, was meant by the other bust? Was it not, in deliberate contrast to the other, left to represent the pagans, as excluded from the Christian world? On the reverse of the *Urbs Roma* coins appear the she-wolf and twins, the miraculous beast of the ancient foundation legend. Above the twins gleam the stars of the Dioscuri, and above the picture hover unseen the divine ancestors, Mars and Rhea, and behind them the shadowy form of Jupiter, throned on the clouds, and the Pantheon of pagan Rome. On the commemorative coins of larger module frightened shepherds draw nigh to the cave of the twins and by their lively gestures announce to one another the wondrous event. Is not this the counterpart of the shepherds of Bethlehem in the New Testament scene?

This involuntary reverence of Constantine for the Roman past gave the guardians of the great tradition other opportunities of flying the old flags before the eyes of the peoples of the Empire. We have already spoken of the example of the imperial cult, stripped, it is true, of its wildly pagan character, but yet preserved intact. On a commemorative coin of the Roman mint, probably struck for the New Year of one of Constantine's last years, Constantine is represented as Jupiter,

while one of the Caesars, his sons, in the guise of Bacchus, the
world-conqueror, brings him an emblem of victory.[1] When
Constantine died in A.D. 337 his sons acquiesced in the decision
of the Senate to apotheosize him in the old style.[2] There was
no other way in which the title of *divus*, 'the divine', could be
bestowed on the deceased ruler. The obverses, it is true, of the
coins struck to commemorate the consecration deliberately
give only the abbreviation $d(i)v(us)$, while the reverses completely avoid the theme and show the heavenward ascent of
the Emperor, with no more than the words 'to his honoured
memory'. But this is another case of what we observed in the
inscription of Hispellum. The imperial cult remains; only such
forms as offend Christian sentiment are a little veiled.[3] As the
scenes of ascent dedicated to the *ven(erandae) mem(oriae)* were
struck by all mints of the Empire, the issue can only have
been ordered by Constantine's successors, whose reputation
was enhanced by the conception in pagan terms of the glorification of their father. On the other hand, we happen to have
a piece of evidence surviving which shows that the Senate did
not conceive of the 'consecration' of Constantine with this
Christian twist to it, but in the original significance. The
Senate had the new *divus* represented within the ether, seated
on the crescent of the sky[4]—the usual way of representing all
regnatores poli who had risen from lordship on earth to lordship
in heaven.[5] Though the Christian courtiers naturally shut their
eyes to this symbolic glorification and raised no objections to

[1] See my arguments in *Num. Közl.* xli, 1942, 9 = *J.R.S.* xxxvii, 1947, 15.
[2] Eutr. x. 8. 2: 'Atque inter divos meruit referri.' Vgl. Victor, *Caes.* 41. 5:
'pro conditore seu deo habitus.' Examples of the title *Divus* on inscriptions
have been collected by E. Ferrero, *Dizionario epigr.* ii. 651.
[3] The words *venerandae memoriae—princeps* were applied to Constantine by
Firmicus Maternus, *Mathes.* i. 10. 13. On a later group of small coins from
Gaul *divo* is written out in full, whilst on the reverse it is balanced by the
Cross. See J. Maurice, *Num. Const.*, i, pl. 22, 23; 4. 25 and pl. 6, 27. On
these questions see P. Franchi de' Cavallieri, *Mélanges d'arch. et d'hist.* xxxvi,
1916–17, 256 ff.; N. Láng, *Károlyi Árpád Emlékkönyv*, 1933, 332; P. Lejay,
Revue de Philol. xxxvi, 1912, 201 f.; A. Kaniuth, op. cit. 69; Th. Mommsen,
Ges. Schriften, viii, 44 f.
[4] Euseb. *Vita Const.* 4. 69 (p. 146. 19 ff. Heikel).
[5] I hope to deal with this question more fully in publishing the Arch of
Galerius at Salonica.

its pagan character,[1] there can be no doubt that such deifying of a man is in stark contrast to the teaching of Christ. Apart from these signs of life in Roman paganism that were reflected afar, in Rome, in the inner circle of the city, the life of the old cults flowed steadily on—all the imperial edicts against them had as good as no effect. To take just one case: it is not merely by accident that not once in Constantine's lifetime was an issue with the emblem of Christ put out by the mint of Rome.

After the imperial house had left Rome, the Senate again, as once of old, was the sole representative of its interests. The Emperor for his part recognizes, even if only as restricted to Rome, the ancient rank of the body, and this gives its activities a new emphasis. The Senate was therefore able to represent, as in the past but with far higher power, the moral traditions of Rome, the *mos maiorum*, which may be compared to our own conception of legitimacy, in contrast to the claims of the Christian Church to total domination.

As we have already observed, the municipal elements introduced into the Senate by Constantine soon suffered a change in the atmosphere of Rome or vanished completely; the traditions of the old families continued to be as decisive as ever. Some of these families became related to the dynasty. Eutropia, the young sister of Constantine, married Virius Nepotianus and lived with him in Rome.[2] Popilianus Nepotianus, consul A.D. 336, was the issue of this marriage. Another man to become related to the Emperor was Ceionius Julianus Camenius, governor of Rome in A.D. 333 to 334.[3] Of such men one must expect that the Christian tide bore them away with it. Towards the end of the reign of Constantine we find Christians among the consuls. Flavius Gallicanus, consul in A.D. 330, was probably a Christian;[4] so too was one of the

[1] Of the father of Constantine his minor court poet Optatianus Porphyrius writes, *carm.* 8. 19 f.: 'et res Constanti nunc exerit inclita fama, aucta stirpe pia, voto accumulata perenni, sancta suas sedes ad mentis gaudia migrat aetherio residens felix in cardine mundi.'

[2] O. Seeck, *RE.* vi, 1915. According to W. Ensslin, *Annuaire de l'Inst. de Philol. et d'Hist. Orient.* ii, 1933–4 (Mélanges Bidez), 369, he was consul A.D. 336.

[3] O. Seeck, *RE.* iii, 1859, no. 19; H. v. Schoenebeck, op. cit. 73 ff.

[4] O. Seeck, *RE.* vii. 668, no. 7.

consuls of A.D. 331, Ablabius, a close confidant of the Emperor who from A.D. 329 at latest till his death filled the post of imperial prefect, *praefectus praetorio*, at his side,[1] and again, in A.D. 333, Zenophilus. But beside the Emperor and the members of his family the families of great Roman land-owners had from A.D. 312 on taken a regular share in holding the consulship; and that office, even in the late Roman age, continued to be the highest representative honour. It shows the partiality for the Senate that Constantine carried over from his *optimus princeps* days. The consul of A.D. 330 was Tullianus Symmachus Valerius, who probably took the same kind of part in the development of the pagan reaction as his descendant did later at its moment of supreme effort.[2] Amnius Bassus, one of the consuls who gave their names to the year A.D. 331, was a son-in-law of Amnius Anicius Julianus, consul in A.D. 322, and came from circles worthy of that out-standing family. He never became a Christian—that was left to his son.[3] The Anicii gave one of the two consuls to the year A.D. 334 whose many names often recur singly in the roll of the most distinguished Romans of later generations—Amnius Manius Caesonius Nicomachus Anicius Paulinus Honorius.[4] Ceionius Rufius Albinus,[5] who entered upon office at the New Year of A.D. 335, was the son of the consul of A.D. 311 and 314. His father is designated in one inscription[6] 'most religious', *religiosissimus*; another[7] inscription calls him *philosophus*. In all probability he was a Neoplatonist: that is to say, a pagan by conviction. We know something of his literary activities. His

[1] J.-R. Palanque, *Essai sur la préfecture du prétoire du Bas-Empire*, 1933, 7 ff. ; O. Seeck, *RE*. i. 103 ff. ; H. v. Schoenebeck, op. cit. 73.

[2] O. Seeck, *RE*. ivA, 1141, and, in opposition to him, Ensslin, *RE*. viiA, 998. I do not understand why this first Symmachus of whom we know should have been one of those barbarians whom Constantine distinguished with the consulship; see Amm. xxi. 10. 8 and cf. O. Seeck, *Hermes*, xli, 1906, 533. Seeck himself admits that his wife came of a noble family. In my opinion, these barbarians whom Constantine honoured with the consulship—only the 'suffect', be it noted—are rather to be looked for among the soldiers than among men who passed through a great civil career.

[3] O. Seeck, *RE*. i. 2199 ff. and 3. 108, no. 18.

[4] O. Seeck, *RE*. i. 2199, no. 28.

[5] O. Seeck, *RE*. iii. 1860, no. 21. For his ancestry see ibid. 1861 f.

[6] *C.I.L.* vi. 4707 = Dessau 1213.   [7] Ibid. vi. 1708 = Dessau 1222.

works on dialectics and geometry may have been designed to contribute to the rhetorical education of the time. After the consulship he became city prefect of Rome, and he succeeded in inducing the Emperor to give back to the Senate the election of praetors and quaestors—offices once important but now implying material burdens rather than honour. For this token of imperial favour that he secured the Senate awarded him exceptional distinctions.[1] What interests us is the fact that at the very end of his life Constantine could still flatter the Senate. Finally, Fabius Tatianus, who held the consulship in A.D. 337, came of a very illustrious senatorial family.[2] In these last years of Constantine most of the city prefects of Rome were pagan aristocrats,[3] for example, Petronius Probianus, A.D. 329 to 331,[4] a great friend of literature, whose family, related by marriage to the Anicii, played so great a part in the generations following. There were also Anicius Paulinus and Ceionius Rufius Albinus, whom we have already met. One more evidence of this devotion of Constantine, half deliberate, half unconscious, to the great traditions of Rome is to be seen in the fact that he revived for his half-brother the office of 'censor' and bestowed the rank of 'patrician' on his relatives.[5]

The supreme self-confidence with which the Roman aristocracy, now thrown back on its own resources, fought for its old rights is shown by the events that took place after the death of Constantine. Eusebius is undoubtedly answering pagan critics when he attempts to prove that the ancient capital mourned the dead Emperor in all sincerity.[6] He tells

[1] O. Seeck, *Hermes*, xix. 1884, 186 f.
[2] E. Groag, *RE.* vi. 1869, no. 149 and 2848, no. 28; M. Fluss and A. Stein, *RE.* xiv. 281 f.   [3] H. v. Schoenebeck, op. cit. 73 ff.
[4] O. Seeck, *RE.* i. 2203, no. 36; see also 2201 f.
[5] E. Stein, *Gesch. d. spätröm. R.* i. 168; W. Ensslin, *Rheinisches Museum*, N.F. lxxviii. 211; id., *Mélanges Bidez*, 1934, 361 ff., especially 369 f.
[6] See P. Meyer, *Festschrift dem Gymnasium Adolfinum zu Moers zu der am 10 and 11 Aug. d. J. stattfindenden Jubelfeier seines dreihundertjährigen Bestehens gewidmet vom Lehrerkollegium des Gymnasiums Krefeld*, 1882, 23 ff. According to Eusebius, *Vita Const.* 4. 63, the last act of the Emperor before his death was to regale the people of Rome with New Year's presents: Ῥωμαίους μὲν τοὺς τὴν βασιλίδα πόλιν οἰκοῦντας ἐτίμα δόσεσιν ἐτησίαις. But, we may ask, was this a question of supplies of food to the *plebs urbana* or of support to the Christian Churches of Rome?

how[1] 'the baths and the market were closed, the public games and all other entertainments were suspended—everything, in fact, that men do to gladden their lives'. But this was done in obedience to edict, and if, to quote him, 'those who had been engaging in such wild luxury now paced the streets with faces downcast', there is at least this much truth in his statement, that the Christians really did mourn. 'All, with one breath', he continues, 'praised him as the favourite of God, as a man worthy to rule.' Such hymns of praise were regularly sung by the choruses in the amphitheatre at the decease of Emperors, and like them were the acclamations that recognized the sons of the dead Emperor, them and no others, as their lords.[2] Customary, too, was the representation, already mentioned, of the new *divus* sitting on the crescent of the sky. All the more remarkable and worthy of attention is the fact that the Roman people demonstrated in the streets, demanding that Constantine be buried, not in the new capital, but in Rome.[3] Such expressions of public opinion derived as much from the old Roman self-confidence as from the recently accentuated authority of Rome. Here a development finds its way to the surface, on which Constantine can hardly have counted.

What conception Constantine formed of the position of Rome after the foundation of his anti-Rome is shown by the propaganda of the Court. The commemorative coins with the legend *Securitas Romae*,[4] on which two gamesome girls bear the goddess Roma on their shoulders with the artlessness of groups of girls at play on Hellenistic terra-cottas, express the same message as that of the verse-writing prefect of A.D. 332,

[1] Euseb. *Vita Const.* 4. 69.
[2] See the excellent remarks of L. P. Franchi de' Cavallieri, in *Mél. d'arch. et d'hist.* xxxvi, 1916/17, 208.
[3] Euseb. *Vita Const.* 4. 96 (p. 146. 24 f. Heikel): βοαῖς τ' ἐχρῶντο ἱκετηρίαις τὸ σκῆνος τοῦ σφῶν βασιλέως παρ' αὐτοῖς κομίζεσθαι καὶ τῇ βασιλίδι πόλει κατατίθεσθαι. The same account, from a different source, is given by Aurelius Victor, *Caes.* 41. 17: 'Funus relatum in urbes sui nominis. Quod sane populus Romanus aegerrime tulit, quippe cuius armis legibus clementi imperio quasi novatam urbem Romam arbitraretur.' (This is just a piece of flattery to please his son, who had just become Emperor.)
[4] See my paper, *Num. Közl.* xli, 1942, 3, note 4.

Optatianus Porphyrius,[1] after the defeat of the Goths in the
territory of the Sarmatians: 'So mayst Thou, while the swords
are bent to ploughshares, enjoy full rest in Thy snowy citadel.
The sister Rome, the jewel of the Pontus, only serves to exalt
the Tuscan Rome, which we behold with our own eyes.' Rome
may thus 'rest on her laurels', may, like a veteran after his
discharge, enjoy the rays of the setting sun.

But when Constantine gave his sanction to the supremacy
of Rome over every other city, he was also permitting the
incorporation of the conception of the old Republican 'ruling
city' in the organization of his new Christian Empire. Up to
the end of the century, it is true, Constantinople, step by step,
gains the rank of Rome. At its head comes to stand a
praefectus urbi instead of a *proconsul*, its Senate and bishop
enjoy the same rank as the Roman. But it is just at this time
that the Empire breaks in two; and, for the West, Rome still
remains Rome. Thus the idea of sovereignty in the Rome of
the Middle Ages rests on the constitutional reforms of Constantine, when, willy-nilly, he had built the pagan tradition of
Rome into the spiritual foundations of his Christian Empire.

And he was not limiting himself to the realm of pure theory
when he permitted the Roman Senate to retain in his new
order its position as the supreme class of society. The new
Court dignitaries of non-senatorial rank never rested from
their strivings until they had won the title of *vir clarissimus*,
until towards the middle of the century they had all, one by
one, attained it. But as soon as the highest imperial functions
were borne by *viri clarissimi* they stood automatically open to
the senatorial families. Thus the aristocratic society that had
been laid on the shelf in the third century, though still excluded
from the now barbarian army, again reached the pinnacle of
the imperial administration. As a result of this they succeeded
not only in retaining but even in increasing their vast landed

[1] Optat. Porph. *Carm.* 18. 32 ff.: 'Sic istis cultus in rem curvantibus enses
te nivea iuvat arce frui. Ponti decus auget, Roma soror, veteres Tuscos, quos
ore tuemur.' The blessed restfulness of the peace established by Constantine
is also celebrated in *carm.* 5. 15 f. Better still: Nazar. paneg. 35. 3–4:
'Placidam quippe rerum quietem et profundum urbi otium gentis perdomitae
condiderunt. Vacat remissioribus animis delectamenta pacis adhibere.'

possessions and thus grew more and more to be a State within the State.

All this time we must not forget that the overwhelming majority of this society was pagan. So it was that the extraordinary strength of the social and economic position of the Senate contributed its share to that reaction of the national paganism of Rome against the attempts of Constantine to impose Christianity on it, which gradually grew in power, until in the course of a few decades it rose to be a movement of genuine importance in world history.

NOTES

1 (p. 5). An excellent selection of the literature on the subject, accompanied by judicious criticism, has recently been given by N. H. Baynes in 'Constantine the Great and the Christian Church', *Proceedings of the British Academy*, xv, 1929–31; a survey of works published in the last decade will be found in my article in *Pisciculi*, Franz Joseph Dölger dargeboten, 1939, 1 ff. W. Ensslin reports on the latest articles in *Klio*, xxxiii, 1941, 355 ff. I have been unable to make use of a few recent works, such as P. Brezzi, 'La politica religiosa di Costantino', *Studi e materiali per la storia d. relig.*, 1941, 37–71; P. Doerfler, 'Der Glaube Konstantins d. Gr.', *Das Hochland*, xxxviii, 1940–1, 22–8. Other results are quoted in the notes as required. The sections of this work that relate to Constantine have already appeared in the Hungarian periodical, *Olasz Szemle*, 1942, 797–836; 1943, 3–59. It gave me great pleasure to notice that J. Vogt reached similar results to mine at the same time in *Zeitschrift für Kirchengeschichte*, 1942, 171–91, dependent, in part, on my earlier researches; cf. also his paper in *Röm. Mitt.* lviii, 1943, 190 ff. I have given a short summary of the theme of this book in 'La conversione di Costantino Roma e pagana', *Estratto da 'Corvina'*, November 1943, 529–44.

2 (p. 5). For the general background see J. Geffcken, *Der Ausgang des griechisch-römischen Heidentums²*, 1929; Fr. Cumont, 'La Théologie solaire du paganisme romain', *Mémoires présentés par divers savants à l'Académie des Inscriptions et Belles-Lettres*, 12. 2. 1913, 447 ff.; id. *Les Religions orientales dans le paganisme romain⁴*, 1929; H. Usener, *Das Weihnachtsfest²*, 1911, 348 ff.; Fr. J. Dölger, *Antike und Christentum*, ii, 1930, 301 ff.; W. Weber, *Die Vereinheitlichung der religiösen Welt (Probleme der Spätantike)*, 1930; F. J. Dölger, *Sol Salutis²*, 1925. A full bibliography of the religious history is given by A. D. Nock, *Cambridge Ancient History*, xii, 1939, 764–6. On syncretism in the religion of Constantine see L. Salvatorelli, *Ricerche religiose*, iv, 1928, 289 ff.; P. Batiffol, *Bulletin d'ancienne littérature et d'archéologie chrétiennes*, iii, 1913, 179 ff.; id., *La Paix Constantinienne³*, 1914, 188 ff.; G. Costa, *Religione e politica nell' impero romano*, 1923, 203 ff.; H. Grégoire, *Revue de l'Université de Bruxelles*, xxxvi, 1930/1, 256 ff.; J. Straub, *Das neue Bild der Antike* (published by H. Berve), ii, 1942, 386 ff., &c.

3 (p. 8). *Appendix Optati*, ed. Ziwsa, no. V = H. v. Soden, 'Urkunden zur Geschichte des Donatismus', *Kleine Texte*, cxxii, 1913, no. 18: '. . . incomprehensibilis pietas dei nostri nequaquam permittit humanam condicionem diutius in tenebris oberrare . . . habeo quippe cognitum multis exemplis, haec eadem ex me ipso metior. Fuerunt enim in me primitus, quae iustitia carere videbantur, nec ulla⟨m⟩ putabam videre supernam potentiam, quae intra secreta pectoris mei gererem . . . sed deus omnipotens in caeli specula residens tribuit, quod non merebar: certe iam neque dici neque enumerari possunt ea, quae caelesti sua in me famulum suum benivolentia concessit.'

4 (p. 10). Since the appearance of the famous book of A. v. Harnack on

the *Mission und Ausbreitung des Christentums in den ersten 3 Jahrhunderten*[4], 1929, countless new evidences of the vitality of Christianity have come to light which prove that the position of the Church about A.D. 300 was considerably stronger than used to be supposed. For example, one of the latest provinces to be Christianized, Pannonia, in that part of it that lies north of the Drave, from which, till recently, absolutely no Christian monuments were known, has in the last few years yielded many new signs of the young Church which, in their origins at least, go back to the age of the Tetrarchy. Cf. Nagy Lajos, *Szent István-Emlékkönyv*, i, 1938, 31 ff.; T. Nagy, *A pannoniai kereszténység története*, Diss. Pann. ii. 12, 31 ff.; A. Alföldi, *Arch. Értesítő*, 1940, 217 ff.; Gy. Török, ibid., 1942, 211 ff.; Gy. Gosztonyi, ibid. 202 ff.; id., *A pécsi Szent Péter székesegyház eredete*, 1939; id., *Arch. Értesítő*, 1944–5, 261 ff.; T. Nagy, ibid. 1944–5, 273 ff., &c.

5 (p. 11). The quotations that I gave in *Pisciculi* to illustrate the position could be multiplied almost at will. I will only cite one particularly characteristic passage from Libanius: he describes how, when Julian was arming against the Persians, the troops that he had brought with him from the West went into battle, invoking their old gods; the Apostate used every means of persuading or compelling those regiments that had served under Constantius II to turn from Christianity and serve the old gods, for all valour and the best weapons are in vain, unless the gods aid; he endeavours, then, by sacrifice, which he performs for himself and his army, to insure the favour of Heaven and, with it, the victory. Liban. *Or.* 18, 166 ff. = vol. ii, 308, Foerst. Cf. G. R. Sievers, *Das Leben des Libanius*, 1868, 108.

The same note echoes from the pagan side in the *Historia Augusta*—but that does not imply any immediate connexion of that sorry compilation with Julian. It is put into the mouth of Marcus Aurelius when on the march against Avidius Cassius; V. Avid. Cass. 8. 3: 'dixisse dicitur (Marcus): non sic deos coluimus, nec sic viximus, ut ille nos vinceret.'

6 (p. 19). That the heavenly powers gave directions in dreams was common property of all ancient faiths; see Th. Hopfner, *Griech.-ägypt. Offenbarungszauber*, ii, 1924, 80 ff. and id. *RE.* xiv. 268 ff. with the literature; L. Friedländer–G. Wissowa, *Darstellungen aus der Sittengeschichte Roms*, iii[10], 1923, 169 ff.; A. J. Festugière, *La Révélation d'Hermès Trismégiste*, i, 1944, 50 ff.; A. Wikenhauser, *Pisciculi*, 1939, 320 ff. Examples from later antiquity could be multiplied. For example, under Constantius II a charge of high treason was brought against a man for dreams that had promised him the throne. Constantius himself attached great importance to his own dreams. See O. Seeck, *Gesch. d. Unterg. d. ant. Welt*, iv. 396 on p. 38, l. 24. The same is true of his pagan opponent, Julian the Apostate, cf. P. Allard, *Julien l'Apostat II*[3], 1910, 217, &c., and of the polished rhetorician of the age, Libanius, cf. J. Geffcken, op. cit. 166 ff. How this age conceived of the intervention of Christ can be well illustrated by a passage in Arnobius, *Adv. nat.* i. 46—only for the *nomen auditum* we must read *signum scriptum*—the same magical potency was attached to both; 'qui (Christus) iustissimis viris etiamnunc inpollutis ac diligentibus sese non per vana insomnia sed per purae

speciem simplicitatis apparet, cuius nomen auditum fugat noxios spiritus, inponit silentium vatibus, haruspices inconsultos reddit, adrogantium magorum frustrari efficit actiones, non horrore ut dicitis nominis sed maioris licentia potestatis.' This idea too is inherited from primitive thoughts of magic; see H. Werner, *Einführung in die Entwicklungspsychologie*[2], 1933, 323. The dream is a means—as it is still in the superstitious strata of our society—for the superhuman powers to announce their will to men; ecstatic visions often have the same significance. For a correct interpretation see L. Binswanger, *Wandlungen in der Auffassung und Deutung des Traumes*, 1928, 107 ff.: 'In dreams there is no question of foreknowledge of a real event, not even of one that the sleeper himself is to bring about, but of the real experience of a definite spiritual tendency. . . . With the prophetic function of dreams positive science will have no more to do. It leaves this field to poetry. . . . Even when "warning" dreams actually occur, they must not be regarded as prophecies, but as continuations, in dream language, of conscious reflections, fears or wishes or, at times, as the emergence of impressions and mental excitements unnoticed or suppressed in waking hours. . . . Even that tendency to look forward and accomplish, in which Maeder sees a frequent function of dreams, does not belong to the field of prophecy in dreams. This tendency to look forward, as Freud emphatically remarked, does not belong to the dream-state as such, but to the thoughts that are latent in sleep. It has as much or little right to be called prophetic as our reason in general—in the sense in which Schopenhauer observes: "Reason itself deserves to be called a prophet: it holds out the future before us as the after-result and effect of our activity of the moment."'

7 (p. 22). F. J. Dölger, *Sphragis*, 1911; id., *Die Sonne der Gerechtigkeit und der Schwarze*, 1919, 19 ff.; H. Lilliebjörn, *Über religiöse Signierungen in der Antike, m. bes. Berücksichtigung der Kreuzsignierung*, Diss., Uppsala, 1933; A.-J. Festugière, *La Révélation d'Hermès Trism.* i. 257, n. 2; A. Alföldi, *Pisciculi*, 17. Of the magical efficacy of the 'true' name of God we shall speak in the Vol. on Valentinian I; meanwhile, cf. G. Bardy, *Recherches de science religieuse*, xviii, 1928, 126 ff., and following him H. Leclerq, *Dictionnaire d'Archéol. chrét.* x. 1, 1931, 1080 f. These names, like other magic words, were often abbreviated and hidden under secret signs; see Th. Hopfner, *RE.*, Suppl. iv, 1183 ff., χαρακτῆρες, in one case complicated cryptograms, in another simple letters; as for example in Plin. *N.H.* 28. 29: 'M. Servilius Nonianus princeps civitatis non pridem in metu lippitudinis, priusquam ipse eam nominaret aliusque ei praediceret, duabus litteris Graecis P A chartam inscriptam circumligatam lino subnectebat collo.' Such letters and monograms were used quite generally as a means of averting evil and driving away disease. Alex. Trall. 2, p. 377 = R. Heim, *Incantamenta magica Graeca Latina* (*Jhb. f. cl. Philol.* Suppl. xix), 1893, 480, no. 57. It is well known how the disciples of Christ and countless others after them used the name of the Redeemer to cast out evil spirits. Cf. *Acta Ap.* 19. 12–16, &c.

I have already pointed out in my paper in the *Pisciculi* that Constantine's battle was not the first case in Roman imperial history in which heavenly

signs and visions had a decisive influence on the Roman or the hostile army;
I quoted the 'miracle of the rain' under Marcus Aurelius as a particularly
significant example. Another instance of characteristic importance is the
description of the battle between Septimius Severus and Pescennius Niger in
Dio Cassius, lxxiv. 7. 6–7. According to this account the army of Pescennius
gained the upper hand by its superior numbers and its more favourable
position and would have achieved a complete victory, had not clouds suddenly gathered in a bright sky and the calm been replaced by a violent storm.
The troops of Severus did not suffer from the storm, which blew the wind
into their backs, while their adversaries received the blast full in their faces
and were thrown into confusion by it. One party saw in the occurrence the
favour of heaven helping them, ὡς καὶ παρὰ τοῦ θείου βοηθουμένοις, while the
other was disturbed by the thought that the gods themselves had turned against
them. It sounds like an anticipation of the description of the battle of the
Frigidus, A.D. 394. It seems that other writers in describing the decisive
battle enlarged on the heavenly signs, emphasizing the favour that the gods
showed to Severus; Herodian, ii. 15. 6, for example, writes: καὶ σημεῖα θείᾳ
προνοίᾳ δόξαντα πολλάκις φανῆναι . . . ἱστορίας τε πολλοὶ συγγραφεῖς καὶ ποιηταὶ
μέτρῳ πλατύτερον συνέταξαν.

8 (p. 22). Lactant. *Div. inst.* iv. 27. I ff. (*Corp. script. eccl. Lat.* xix. 384 ff.):
'quanto terrori sit daemonibus hoc signum, sciet qui viderit quatenus adiurati
per Christum de corporibus quae obsederint fugiant . . . cuius rei non difficilis
est probatio. nam cum diis suis immolant, si adsistat aliquis signatam fron-
tem gerens, sacra nullo modo litant et hoc saepe causa praecipua iustitiam
persequendi malis regibus fuit. cum enim quidam ministrorum nostri sacrifi-
cantibus dominis adsisterent, inposito frontibus signo deos illorum fuga-
verunt, ne possent in visceribus hostiarum futura depingere. quod cum
intellegerent haruspices, instigantibus isdem daemonibus quibus prosecant
conquerentes profanos homines sacris interesse egerunt principes suos in
furorem, ut expugnarent dei templum. . . .'

9 (p. 23). Euseb. *Vita Const.* 2. 7 and 9, &c. This view is shared to-day by
scholars of the most diverse tendencies, for example, Th. Zahn, *Constantin d.
Gr. u. die Kirche*, 1876, 14; O. Seeck, op. cit. i⁴. 57 f. ; H. Koch, *Konstantin der
Grosse und das Christentum*, 1913, 20; K. Bihlmeyer, *Kirchengeschichte auf
Grund des Lehrbuchs von F. X. Funk*, i⁹, 1931, 70, &c. To-day it is surprising,
rather, to find an admirable scholar, Ed. Schwartz, *Göttinger gel. Nachr.*, 1904,
532, daring to write in the spirit of that other excellent scholar, J. Burckhardt,
Die Zeit Constantins d. G. v. 334, that the victor of the battle of the Mulvian
Bridge was 'unprejudiced, like all statesmen of genius'. This change in the
conception of Constantine reflects a general change of direction, which may be
illustrated from the view now taken of Julian the Apostate: 'This prince, whom
people have insisted, at all costs, in making a sceptic, a freethinker, was really a
clairvoyant, who believed that he saw and heard the gods, a devotee, who visited
all the temples and passed a part of his days in prayer': G. Boissier, op. cit., i⁸. 140.

10 (p. 26). 'The moderns find all the expressions of his religious feeling
ambiguous, because they wish to find them so', writes O. Seeck, op. cit. i⁴.

472—much to the point. See also F. Lot, op. cit. 32 f. 'What a shame', writes G. Boissier brilliantly, op. cit. i.[8] 24, 'that, when we have to do with great personalities, who play the chief parts in history, when we try to study their lives and explain their conduct, we are not content to hold to the most natural explanations. Because they have the reputation of being extraordinary men, we will not believe that they have done what everybody else would. We search for hidden reasons for their simplest actions; we attribute to them plots, depths, perfidies of which they were entirely unaware. So it has been with Constantine.'

    11 (p. 28). That is why Christian sentiment has not stamped itself as emphatically on the legislation of Constantine, as many imagine. J. Vogt has recently dealt with the influence of Christianity on Constantine as lawgiver; the older literature is recorded by him, *Festschr. f. L. Wenger*, ii, 1944, 118 ff. He estimates this influence at a higher rate than I do. This admirable scholar sees, it is true, 'that, if we consider how constantly Constantine favoured Christianity, we are inclined to expect the world of Christian thought to have exercised a decisive influence on his legislation, even in questions not connected with the position of Christianity and paganism at law'; he sees too that this did not so fall out (op. cit. 128 f., 138). He admits further that the doctrines of the Stoa, the inheritance of Hellenistic culture, and influences from the East had already with the predecessors of Constantine worked in the same direction as the more humane and social tendency in him (130 and 140 f.), which often finds expression. The defence of the weak against the strong is not only a corollary of the Christian love of your neighbour, but was a necessary consequence of the spirit of the age—he emphasizes this on p. 142; we have only to remember the unfriendliness to the Senate and the care for the poorer orders shown by that pagan with heart of steel, Aurelian. It goes without saying that the Christian priests at the Court of Constantine were often able to get their plans realized in the ordinances of the Emperor. The facilitation of the emancipation of slaves, for example, is really an effect of Christian charity (123). But the treatment of the slave-class remains in general as of old, as Vogt himself points out (130 ff.). It must also be admitted that the codification of the jurisdiction of the bishops (123 ff.) suggests interaction between public law and Christian morality; but he cannot fail to recognize that the competence of the episcopal courts remained very limited. The giving to celibacy of equal rights with the married state (33 and 148) was at that time not only a demand of the Church, but it represented a general movement in that age of recoil from the world, that contempt for the flesh and that admiration for ascetic self-abnegation, that said good-bye to family life. What is left—for example, details of the regulations for divorce (134), the edicts against concubinage (135), the legitimization of marriage (137), the encouragement of the will to make gifts (141 f.), the edicts against the gladiatorial shows (144 f.)—really has a Christian colour but it is thrust into the background by other traits in common with previous legislation and the signs of the new barbarism. Above all, the horrible cruelty of the punishments in the laws of Constantine stands in violent contrast to

the Christian love of neighbour and mercy; see p. 20, n. 4 and p. 31, n. 3. Even if Constantine abolished the punishment of crucifixion, out of superstitious awe of Christ (143), the choice of other punishments in his edicts is enough to make the blood run cold.

12 (p. 37). The extensive literature is most easily accessible in N. H. Baynes, op. cit., see n. 1 above. See also W. Hartmann, 'Konstantin d. Gr. als Christ und Philosoph in seinen Briefen und Erlassen', *Beilage zum Programm d. städt. Gymn. zu Fürstenwalde*, Ostern 1902, 6 ff.; F. Savio, *Civiltà cattolica*, anno 64, 1913, vol. ii. 387 ff., 556 ff., who does not go back to the original authorities, but skilfully recapitulates the results of research; J. R. Palanque, *Byzantion*, x, 1935, 612, &c. The scholars who have regarded the vision of Constantine as an invention or a deception have naturally refused to recognize Constantine's subsequent arrangements in the interest of the Church, and have even discarded the notices in the *Life of Constantine* by Eusebius and the documents relating to the Donatist controversy as forgeries. This view is now completely out of date. See also N. H. Baynes, op. cit. 68 ff., 75 ff. and also my remarks in *Pisciculi*, 1939, 1 ff., and J. Vogt, *Zeitschr. f. Kirchengeschichte*, 1942, 171 ff.

13 (p. 37). A selection of the literature on the programme of Milan, with criticism, may be found in N. H. Baynes, 'Constantine the Great and the Christian Church', 1931, 11 and 69 ff., note 42. Here are a few selections out of many: O. Seeck, *Zeitschr. d. Savigny-Stiftung f. Rechtsgeschichte, rom. Abt.* x, 1889, 182; id., *Zeitschr. f. Kirchengesch.* xii, 1891, 381 ff. and *Geschichte des Untergangs der antiken Welt*, i⁴, 498 f.; H. Hülle, *Die Toleranzerlasse der römischen Kaiser*, 1895; E. Stein, *Geschichte des spätrömischen Reiches*, i, 1928, 141, note 3, and *Catholic Historical Review*, xxi, 1935, 131; P. Batiffol, *Le Correspondant*, 10 March 1913, 839 ff. and id., *La Paix Constantinienne³*, 1914, 230 ff.; J. Wittig, 19. *Supplementband d. Röm. Quartalschrift*, 1913, 40 ff.; K. Bihlmeyer, *Theol. Quartalschrift*, xcvi, 1914, 65 ff., 198 ff.; G. L. Perugi, *Roma e l'Oriente*, anno 3, vol. vi, 1913, 273 ff.; R. Pichon, *Revue des deux mondes*, lxxxiii, 1913, 340 ff.; E. Galli, *La scuola cattolica*, anno 41, vol. ii, 1913, 39 ff.; F. Meda, *Rassegna nazionale*, anno 35, vol. clxxxix, 1913, 473 ff.; W. Schnyder, 'Die Anerkennung der christlichen Kirche von Seiten des röm. Staates unter Konstantin d. Grossen' (*Jahresbericht der kantonalen höheren Lehranstalten in Luzern*, 1912–13); I. A. Heikel, *De Constantini imperatoris scriptis edendis*, 1916, 17 ff.; J. R. Knipfing, *Zeitschrift f. Kirchengeschichte*, xl, 1922, 206 ff., and *Catholic Historical Review*, N.S. iv, 1925, 483 ff.; H. Florin, *Untersuchungen zur diocletianischen Christenverfolgung*, Diss. 1928, 90 ff.; R. Laqueur, *Epitymbion Swoboda*, 1927, 132 ff.; L. Salvatorelli, *Ricerche religiose*, iv, 1928, 312 f.; E. Caspar, op. cit. i, 1930, 581; H. Grégoire, *Revue de l'Université de Bruxelles*, 1930/1, 263; id., *Byzantion*, vii, 1932, 648 f. and x, 1935, 616 ff.; J. R. Palanque, *Byzantion*, x, 1935, 607 ff.; Ed. Schwartz, *Kaiser Konstantin und die christliche Kirche²*, 1936, 66 ff.

14 (p. 43). See *Pisciculi*, 5. Since writing my text I see that O. Voetter, in *Num. Zeitschr.* li, 1918, 187, regards this medallion as contemporary with the series of three types from Treves. To the determination of date

4996   K

I have an important observation to add. The reverse is identical with the type of a 'follis' of Maxentius from Ostia, *Adlocutio Aug.*; I shall prove this in the *Cahiers d'archéologie*, with illustration. The same engraver who made the bronze of Maxentius also engraved the die for the silver medallion of Constantine. The mint of Ostia was transferred to Arles soon after the defeat of Maxentius (see L. Laffranchi, *Revue Belge de Numismatique*, lxiii, 1921, 7 ff.), and it is therefore most unlikely that either the die or the style, which soon underwent a change, can have been in use later than the years immediately succeeding the battle of the Mulvian Bridge. Cf. also Firm. Matern., *De errore prof. relig.* 21. 4.

15 (p. 48). A. Piganiol, *L'Empereur Constantin*, 1932, 128: 'Unfortunately we cannot date exactly Constantine's first law on the Sabbath rest. The text that we possess was posted up in Sardinia, in March or July A.D. 321, but a long interval often elapsed between the issue of an edict and its publication in the provinces. On the other hand, this text seems to be correcting an older law and softening its prescriptions. Constantine had ordered that the tribunals should be closed on the Sunday. Now he goes back on that order and decides that they shall remain open for enfranchisements and emancipations. He also decides to exempt the peasants from compulsory idleness, in order that they may be able to take advantage of the fine weather that Providence gives them. We incline to think that the first measures, taken by Constantine in relation to the Sunday rest, were earlier than A.D. 321. A curious text of an inscription from Pannonia, unfortunately not dated, *C.I.L.* iii. 4121, tells us that, in this province, Constantine fixed the Sunday as market day, perhaps in order to make it easier to break off hard work.'

16 (p. 51). E. Caspar, *Geschichte des Papsttums*, i, 1930, 124: 'During this first residence of Constantine in Rome in A.D. 312, occurred an imperial gift of great splendour, of importance for the state of the Bishop of Rome, the assignment of the *domus Faustae*, the Lateran, to be the Bishop's residence; for, only a few months later, this palace of the consort of the Emperor was the meeting-place of the Roman Synod of A.D. 313. That Constantine first assigned it for this purpose is not recorded and not probable; when Miltiades assembled the Synod there, it is obvious that he was already master of the Lateran.' See also L. Duchesne, *Histoire ancienne de l'Église*, ii, 1907, 110, n. 3, to the same effect.

17 (p. 51). A. Piganiol, op. cit. 113; H. v. Schoenebeck, op. cit. 88 ff.; see also *Liber pontificalis*, ed. Duchesne, p. 191 ff.; Cabrol-Leclercq, *Dictionnaire d'archéologie chrétienne*, viii, 1545; H. Jordan–Chr. Huelsen, *Topographie der Stadt Rom*, iii², 1907, 243; Ph. Lauer, *Le Palais de Latran*, 1911; H. Lietzmann, *Petrus und Paulus in Rom²*, 1927, 189 ff.; Th. Klauser, *Forschungen und Fortschritte*, xiii, 1937, 57 f.; id., 'Vom Heroon zur Märtyrerbasilika' (*Kriegsvorträge der Friedrich-Wilhelm-Universität, Bonn a. Rh.*, Heft lxii), 1942, 5 ff.; M. Armellini–C. Cecchelli, *Le chiese di Roma*, i², 1942, 121 ff.; further literature in A. Piganiol, *Histoire de Rome*, 1939, 478.

18 (p. 53). Lactant. *Epitome divin. instit.* 49. 1–4: 'atquin religio sola est, in qua libertas domicilium conlocavit. res est enim praeter ceteras voluntaria

nec inponi cuiquam necessitas potest, ut colat, quod non vult. potest aliquis forsitan simulare, non potest velle. denique cum metu tormentorum aliqui aut cruciatibus victi ad execranda sacrificia consenserint, numquam ultro faciunt quod necessitate fecerunt, sed data rursus facultate ac reddita libertate referunt se ad deum eumque precibus et lacrimis placant agentes non voluntatis quam non habuerunt, sed necessitatis quam pertulerunt paenitentiam, et venia satisfacientibus non negatur. quid ergo promovet qui corpus inquinat, quando inmutare non potest voluntatem?'

19 (p. 54). Lactant. *De mort. pers.* 48. 2: 'Quo quicquid divinitatis in sede caelesti, nobis atque omnibus qui sub potestate nostra sunt constituti, placatum ac propitium possit existere' = Euseb. *H.E.* x. 5. 4: ὅπως ὅ τί ποτέ ἐστιν θειότητος καὶ οὐρανίου πράγματος, ἡμῖν καὶ πᾶσι τοῖς ὑπὸ τὴν ἡμετέραν ἐξουσίαν διάγουσιν εὐμενὲς εἶναι δυνηθῇ. See also Lactant. op. cit. 48. 3 = Euseb. *H.E.* x. 5. 5 and Lactant. op. cit. 48. 11 = Euseb. *H.E.* x. 5. 13. It is especially important that the same thought is beginning to glimmer in Galerius' edict of toleration. Lactant. *De mort. pers.* 34. 5: 'Unde [christiani] iuxta hanc indulgentiam nostram debebunt deum suum orare pro salute nostra et rei publicae ac sua, ut undique versum res publica perstet incolumis et securi vivere in sedibus suis possint.'

20 (p. 57). See, for example, R. Pichon, *Revue des deux mondes*, lxxxiii, 1913, 344; 'It is true that this theological vocabulary of the Edict is philosophical rather than religious, deistic rather than Christian: with its quite general terms and its vague epithets, "divinity", "divine power", "heavenly favour", it might suit a disciple of Plato or of Zeno just as well as a worshipper of Christ; it might even suit a pagan, at least one of those pagans, so numerous at the time, who considered the gods of paganism as so many different emanations of a single and unique supreme Being. It is quite close to the phraseology that we shall meet later in avowed pagans, like that Maximus of Madaura, who corresponded with Saint Augustine. The imperial style, to put it in a word, has nothing in it specially Christian. But that does not mean to say that the thought is not Christian.'

21 (p. 59). Κωνσταντίνῳ λάμποντι Ἡλίου δίκην. The details may be found in the valuable paper of Th. Preger in *Hermes*, xxxvi, 1901, 457 ff. See also L. Bréhier, *Rev. hist.* cxix, 1915, 263 f.; D. Lathoud, *Échos d'Orient*, xxiii, 1924, 296 ff.; Fr. J. Dölger, *Sol salutis*², 1925, 66 ff.; F. Stähelin, *Zeitschrift f. Schweizerische Geschichte*, xvii, 1937, 411 ff.; Joh. Straub, op. cit., 130 f. and 247, n. 249; A. Kaniuth, *Die Beisetzung Konstantins des Grossen*, 1941, 77 f. On the inscription see Th. Reinach, *Revue des Études grecques*, ix, 1896, 38; F. Dölger, *Zeitschrift f. Kirchengeschichte*, lvi, 1937, 23, n. 37. This cannot have been any kind of municipal dedication, as Fr. J. Dölger supposes, but a document planned by the Emperor and originating in the Court. Whether there was a cross on the globe in Constantine's hand is doubtful; the globe with the cross only appears normally later, about A.D. 400; see my remarks in *Acta Archaeologica*, v, 1934, 141 f.; but it is not out of the question, for we find the globe, resting on the cross, as early as A.D. 315 on a silver medallion of Ticinum. See also D. Lathoud, op. cit. 306.

22 (p. 59). This has been very clearly realized by V. Schultze, *Geschichte des griechisch-römischen Heidentums*, i, 1887, 39 f.: 'No man of any intelligence could fail to see that a sudden and violent divorce of paganism from the ancient State and the public life of the Empire would have thrown that Empire into the most perilous convulsions and would have seriously endangered the existence of the new imperial constitution. . . . The utmost that a Christian Emperor, who was in earnest with his attempts to spread Christianity, could do under the existing circumstances was to depress and gradually limit paganism, as far as possible by way of administrative measures and in a form that either avoided violent action or else adroitly disguised it.—This is the line that Constantine's home policy takes. It took that direction from the beginning, but, of course, it found less decided expression in the earlier years than towards the end of the Emperor's reign. Fixed as far as its general goal was concerned, in its practical application it was bound to be a policy that took each case on its merits.'

23 (p. 69). *Incerti paneg. Constantino Aug. d.* 25. 4, p. 309, Guil. Baehrens: 'Merito igitur tibi, Constantine, et nuper senatus signum dei et paulo ante Italia scutum et coronam, cuncta aurea, dedicarunt ut conscientiae debitum aliqua ex parte relevarent. Debetur enim et saepe debebitur et divinitati simulacrum aureum et virtuti scutum et corona pietati.' H. Lietzmann, *Sitzungsber. d. Preuss. Akad.*, 1937, 267, is wrong, for neither statues of gods nor shields, like the *clipeus virtutis*, were normally offered as a special tax at Jubilees, just to be melted down. Others, like M. Besnier, *L'Empire romain*, 1937, 360, n. 110, wrongly identify this pagan manifestation of senatorial feeling with the statue of imperial origin, which holds an ensign with the sign of Christ.

24 (p. 70). It is a mistake for scholars to attribute this shadowy deism to Constantine himself; the distinguished historian, A. Piganiol, op. cit. 83, does so among others. The right connexion of events was realized by G. Boissier, op. cit. 45 f., 50 ff. Very true also is Boissier's comment (op. cit. 356): 'In the panegyric of A.D. 313, eight months after the battle of the Mulvian Bridge, the orator speaks, in terms that betray embarrassment and deliberate vagueness, of the supreme god, creator of the world, who sits beyond the sky and who, while he leaves the *dii minores* to deal with the ordinary affairs of men, has deigned to reveal himself to Constantine', *Paneg.* xii. 2. 4–5; 13. 2; 26. 1; without doubt, there is reference here to a vision. These expressions of feeling are judged in our sense by Joh. Straub, op. cit. 99 and 101.

25 (p. 72). Dessau, *Inscr. Lat. sel.* 694. My view was anticipated by V. Schultze, *Zeitschrift f. Kirchengesch.* vii, 1885, 350: 'On the other hand, the deistic colouring of the inscription shows . . . that something was known of Constantine's inclination in religion towards Christianity and that it was thought advisable to take some account of it.' See also O. Seeck, *Gesch. d. Unterg.* i⁴. 495; Joh. Straub, op. cit. 101; H. v. Schoenebeck, op. cit. 24. In order to understand *instinctu divinitatis* it is worth while illustrating the phraseology by a few examples. Cf., for example: Cic. *Tusc.* 1. 64: 'ut ego

poëtam grave plenumque carmen sine caelesti aliquo mentis instinctu putem fundere' (cf. *pro Archia* 8. 18: 'poëtam quasi divino quodam spiritu afflari'). Cic. *De divin.* i. 6. 12: 'Est enim vis et natura quaedam, quae . . . aliquo instinctu inflatuque divino futura praenuntiat.' Ibid. i. 18. 34: 'oracla . . . quae instinctu divino adflatuque funduntur.' Ibid. i. 31. 66: 'cum a corpore animus abstractus divino instinctu concitatur.' Val. Max. i. 6, ext. 3: 'dearum instinctu'. Ibid. i. 8. 10: 'inpulsu capti numinis instincta virgo.' Apul. *Met.* 11. 26: 'deae potentis instinctu.' Ulpianus, l. vii. de off. procons. = *Mosaicarum et Romanarum legum coll.* xv. 2. 5: 'instinctu deorum.' Lactant. *Instit. divin.* iv. 27. 12: 'ecce aliquis instinctu daemonis percitus dementit.' Id., *De mort. pers.* 3. 2: 'ad persequendum iustum populum instinctu daemonum incitatus est.' Firmic. Matern. *De errore profan. relig.* 21. 5: 'Tu Christe . . . venerando instinctu hoc nobis denuntias per prophetas.'

Ten years later we hear out of the mouth of Constantine himself that he νεύματι καὶ συνεργείᾳ τοῦ κρείττονος, that is to say, *instinctu divinitatis*, had conquered his enemies. Euseb. *Vita Const.* ii. 12; attention to this agreement was called by P. Batiffol, *La Paix Constantinienne*[3], 1914, 333, n. 1. 'Sol' on the Arch of Constantine: H. P. L'Orange, *Der spätantike Bildschmuck des Konstantinbogens*, 1939, 57, 126 ff. and especially, 176 f. The wall-paintings of the Basilica of Junius Bassus might have told us how the Christians depicted the battle of the Mulvian Bridge, were they not lost; if one could see on them how the severed head of Maxentius was presented to Constantine, the miracle of Christ must have been represented earlier in the series. On these paintings, see G. B. de Rossi, *Bullettino arch. cristiana*, 1871, 27.

26 (p. 76). So A. Piganiol, op. cit. 126 ff. Piganiol rightly sees that 'this prohibition is directed, in the first place, against magic', but, in my opinion, the *sacrificia domestica* have no other meaning at all. There is no question of anything but the mastering of the passion for magic that raged in Rome, which brought Valentinian I later into violent conflict with the Senate. Further, the edict, *Cod. Theod.* xvi. 10. 1, which is connected with these prohibitions, is quite clearly and unmistakably restricted to the *haruspices*. It is not allowed to suppose with Piganiol, on the strength of this passage, that 'it is possible that the worship of idols, at least in domestic sanctuaries, was also condemned' (op. cit. 127). That the *haruspices* were actually called on to play a part in intrigues against the Emperor or, generally, dangerous to the common weal, is shown very vividly by Firmicus Maternus, *Mathes.* ii. 30. 4 and 6. They naturally then conducted their operations in secret; in private houses, in fact. That is why Firmicus, ibid. 10, instructs his pupils: 'Nunquam nocturnis sacrificiis intersis, sive illa publica sive privata dicantur.'

27 (p. 78). *Cod. Theod.* xvi. 10. 1: '. . . ad Maximum (p.u.). Si quid de palatio nostro aut ceteris operibus publicis degustatum fulgure esse constiterit, retento more veteris observantiae quid portendat, ab haruspicibus requiratur et diligentissime scribtura collecta ad nostram scientiam referatur, ceteris etiam usurpandae huius consuetudinis licentia tribuenda, dummodo sacrificiis domesticis abstineant, quae specialiter prohibita sunt. Eam autem denuntiationem adque interpretationem, quae de tactu amphitheatri scribta

est, de qua ad Heraclianum tribunum et mag/istrum/ officiorum scribseras, ad nos scias esse perlatam.' For the date, see Seeck, op. cit. 168. 170.
28 (p. 84). Theoderet. *H.E.* 1. 14 (Constantine's letter on the building of the churches): "Ἕως τοῦ παρόντος χρόνου τῆς ἀνοσίου βουλήσεως καὶ τυραννίδος τοὺς ὑπηρέτας τοῦ Σωτῆρος Χριστοῦ διωκούσης. . . . Νυνὶ δὲ τῆς ἐλευθερίας ἀποδοθείσης, καὶ τοῦ δράκοντος ἐκείνου ἀπὸ τῆς τῶν κοινῶν διοικήσεως θεοῦ τοῦ μεγίστου προνοίᾳ, ἡμέτερᾳ δὲ ὑπηρεσίᾳ ἐκδιωχθέντος.... See also Firm. Matern. *De errore profan. relig.* 21. 2 (on the orphic Dionysos): 'Ipse est basiliscus et scorpio, qui fidelium securis vestigiis premitur: ipse malitiosus anguis, cuius caput quaerit decepta mortalitas: ipse tortuosus draco, qui hamo ducitur, qui captivus includitur.'
29 (p. 89). Euseb. *Vita Const.* 2. 60 (p. 65 f. Heikel): Πλὴν ἕκαστος ὅπερ πείσας ἑαυτὸν ἀναδέδεκται, τούτῳ τὸν ἕτερον μὴ καταβλαπτέτω· ὅπερ θάτερος εἶδέν τε καὶ ἐνόησεν, τούτῳ τὸν πλησίον εἰ μὲν γενέσθαι ὠφελείτω, εἰ δ' ἀδύνατον παραπεμπέτω. ἄλλο γὰρ ἐστι ⟨τὸ⟩ τὸν ὑπὲρ ἀθανασίας ἆθλον ἑκουσίως ἐπαναιρεῖσθαι, ἄλλο τὸ μετὰ τιμωρίας ἐπαναγκάζειν. ταῦτα εἶπον, ταῦτα διεξῆλθον μακρότερον ἢ ὁ τῆς ἐμῆς ἐπιεικείας ἀπαιτεῖ σκοπός, ἐπειδὴ τὴν τῆς ἀληθείας ἀποκρύψασθαι πίστιν οὐκ ἐβουλόμην, μάλισθ' ὅτι τινὲς ὡς ἀκούω φασὶ τῶν ναῶν περιῃρῆσθαι τὰ ἔθη καὶ τοῦ σκότους τὴν ἐξουσίαν· ὅπερ συνεβούλευσα ἂν πᾶσιν ἀνθρώποις, εἰ μὴ τῆς μοχθηρᾶς πλάνης ἡ βίαιος ἐπανάστασις ἐπὶ βλάβῃ τῆς κοινῆς σωτηρίας ἀμέτρως ταῖς ἐνίων ψυχαῖς ἐμπεπήγει.
30 (p. 91). 'Vota orbis et urbis, senatus et populi Romani, vicennaliis et tricennaliis Augusti, (sc., susceptis).' The imperial obverses, connected with this reverse, have been collected by H. v. Schoenebeck, op. cit. 146, together with a minor variety, with *multis felicibus* instead of *Augusti* on the reverse. In the illustration in J. Maurice, op. cit. i, pl. 8. 14, the reading of exergue seems to be MRS, not AQS; it is possible, then, that these medallions were struck in Rome and other mints. See also O. Ulrich-Bansa, *Note sulla zecca di Aquileia Romana*, 1936, 29 ff. and pl. 11. 7–11. The explanation why these figures of dedication are inscribed on a column may, perhaps, be found in the passage of Suetonius, *Div. Jul.* 85, where, in recounting the events following the death of Caesar, he illustrates the attitude of the 'plebs' thus: 'postea solidam columnam prope viginti pedum lapidis Numidici in foro statuit inscripsitque PARENTI PATRIAE. apud eam longo tempore *sacrificare, vota suscipere*, controversias quasdam interposito per Caesarem iure iurando distrahere perseveravit.' The custom may have begun here and so continued.
31 (p. 95). Lactant. *De mort. pers.* 7. 8–10: 'Huc accedebat infinita quaedam cupiditas aedificandi, non minor provinciarum exactio in exhibendis operariis et artificibus et plaustris omnibusque quaecumque sint fabricandis operibus necessaria. Hic basilicae, hic circus, hic moneta, hic armorum fabrica, hic uxori domus, hic filiae. Repente magna pars civitatis exciditur. Migrabant omnes cum coniugibus ac liberis quasi urbe ab hostibus capta. Et cum perfecta haec fuerant cum interitu provinciarum, "non recte facta sunt," aiebat, "alio modo fiant." Rursus dirui ac mutari necesse erat iterum fortasse caesura. Ita semper dementabat, Nicomediam studens urbi Romae coaequare.'

$\mathcal{N}otes$ 135

32 (p. 97). F. Lot, op. cit. 42, writes very wisely: 'The ancient city of
Byzantium had till then played a very secondary role, in spite of the theory
that attributes to fine geographical positions what they call "a fateful"
value.' In point of fact, excellence of position is not, in itself, sufficient: the
part played by any particular position may vary with the changing political
and military conditions, one moment unimportant, dominating the next.
There is an excellent passage in Ed. Schwartz, *Kaiser Konstantin und die
christliche Kirche*[2], 1936, 85: 'Aurelian, the precursor of Constantine, was
still thinking of raising Rome to the position of capital in his new Empire;
Constantine would be content with nothing less than the foundation of a new
city; in this, he entered into the immediate succession of Alexander and the
Diadochi, of the Hellenistic monarchy, in fact. Although he was a Westerner
and owed his first elevation and his last deciding victories to Western troops,
he yet transferred his capital to the Greek East, where the tradition of the
absolute monarchy had never been interrupted by the "principate" of
Augustus and there were no memories of old Rome to stand in the way of
a universal despotism . . . finally, with splendid acumen, he chose Byzantium,
with its incomparable position for commerce and for war. . . . She was designed
from the first to be a city of churches. . . .'

33 (p. 100). *Cod. Theod.* xiii. 5. 161 (6 Feb. A.D. 380): 'Idem AAA. corpori
naviculariorum. Delatam vobis a divo Constantino et Iuliano principibus
aeternis equestris ordinis dignitatem nos firmamus.' Cf. the law of Valentinian I, *Cod. Theod.* vi. 37. 1: 'Ad Mamertinum p[raefectum] p[raetori]o.
Equites Romani, quos secundi gradus in urbe omnium optinere volumus
dignitatem, ex indigenis Romanis et civibus eligantur, vel his peregrinis,
quos corporatis non oportet adnecti. Et quia vacuos huiusmodi viros esse
privilegiis non oportet, corporalium eos iniuriarum et prosecutionum formido
non vexet, ab indictionibus quoque, quae senatorium ordinem manent, habe-
buntur immunes.' A. Stein, *Der römische Ritterstand*, 1927, 457 ff., has a short
treatment of these attempts at reform. But it is not correct that these new
knights are the 'noble youth'. A. v. Sallet, *Zeitschr. f. Num.* iii, 1876, 129,
and, following him, K. Hönn, *Konstantin der Grosse*, 1940, 150, thinks that
the *senatus* gold coins were intended for the new Senate of Constantinople;
but this is ruled out both by the chronology and by the parallel emphasis on
the 'knights', as also by the legend of the medallion of Treves.

34 (p. 109). Fully discussed by Le duc de Broglie, *L'Église et L'Empire
romain au IV*[e] *s.* i, 1860, 462 ff. Our view agrees with that of the following
scholars: V. Schultze, *Zeitschr. f. Kirchengesch.* viii, 1886, 529 ff.; id. *Gesch.
d. Untergangs d. griech.-röm. Heidentums*, i, 1887, 56 ff.; F. X. Funk, *Kirchengesch. Abhandlungen u. Untersuchungen*, ii, 1899, 10; O. Seeck, *Gesch. d.
Untergangs d. ant. Welt*, i[4]. 61; and N. H. Baynes, 'Constantine the Great',
47, &c. Others try to explain it as an erroneous generalization from special
prohibitions, not as a special general prohibition of sacrifice. See, for example,
C. Carassai, *Archivio della Soc. romana di storia patria*, xxiv, 1901, 33, n. 5;
L. Salvatorelli, *Ricerche religiose*, iv, 1928, 324 f.; H. Lietzmann, *Gesch. d.
alten Kirche*, iii, 1938, 140; L. Duchesne, *Histoire ancienne de l'église*, ii[2].

76 f.; J. Geffcken, op. cit. 93 f. and n. 23. See also F. Martroye's view, which in my opinion is false, in *Bulletin de la Soc. nat. des Antiquaires de France*, 1915, 280 ff. and id. *Rev. historique de droit français et étr.*, 4th ser. ix, 1930, 669 ff., with which H. Grégoire, in *Byzantion*, vii, 1932, 661 ff., agrees; A. Piganiol, op. cit. 142; cf. p. 133, n. 26 above.

35 (p. 109). So G. Boissier, *La Fin du paganisme*, I[8]. 65. Cf. Mommsen, *Strafrecht*, p. 607, n. 2: 'Perhaps, then, this supposed ordinance may rather have been a warning.' In favour of this view is the testimony of Libanius, who knows of no such prohibition on the part of Constantine. It may have been only an edict, issued at the last moment, that never took effect, or just a general threat; *Or.* 30. 6–7, 3, p. 90 F. on Constantine: ἡγησάμενος αὐτῷ λυσιτελεῖν ἕτερόν τινα νομίζειν θεὸν εἰς μὲν τὴν τῆς πολέως περὶ ἣν ἐσπούδασε ποίησιν τοῖς ἱεροῖς ἐχρήσατο χρήμασι, τῆς κατὰ νόμους δὲ θεραπείας ἐκίνησεν οὐδὲ ἕν, ἀλλ' ἦν μὲν ἐν τοῖς ἱεροῖς πενία, παρῆν δὲ ὁρᾶν ἅπαντα τἄλλα πληρούμενα. καταβάσης δὲ τῆς ἀρχῆς ἐπὶ τὸν ἐξ ἐκείνου, . . . οὗτος οὖν ἐν τῷ κελεύεσθαι παρ' αὐτῶν βασιλεύων ἄλλα τε οὐ καλὰ πείθεται καὶ μηκέτ' εἶναι θυσίας.

INDEX

Index 139

ISBN 0–19–	Author	Title
8143567	ALFÖLDI A.	The Conversion of Constantine and Pagan Rome
6286409	ANDERSON George K.	The Literature of the Anglo-Saxons
8228813	BARTLETT & MacKAY	Medieval Frontier Societies
8114222	BROOKS Kenneth R.	Andreas and the Fates of the Apostles
8148348	CAMPBELL J.B.	The Emperor and the Roman Army 31 BC to 235 AD
826643X	CHADWICK Henry	Priscillian of Avila
826447X	CHADWICK Henry	Boethius
8219393	COWDREY H.E.J.	The Age of Abbot Desiderius
8148992	DAVIES M.	Sophocles: Trachiniae
825301X	DOWNER L.	Leges Henrici Primi
8143109	FRAENKEL Edward	Horace
8201540	GOLDBERG P.J.P.	Women, Work and Life Cycle in a Medieval Economy
8140215	GOTTSCHALK H.B.	Heraclides of Pontus
8266162	HANSON R.P.C.	Saint Patrick
8224354	HARRISS G.L.	King, Parliament and Public Finance in Medieval England to 1369
8581114	HEATH Sir Thomas	Aristarchus of Samos
8140444	HOLLIS A.S.	Callimachus: Hecale
8212968	HOLLISTER C. Warren	Anglo-Saxon Military Institutions
8223129	HURNARD Naomi	The King's Pardon for Homicide – before AD 1307
8140401	HUTCHINSON G.O.	Hellenistic Poetry
8142560	JONES A.H.M.	The Greek City
8218354	JONES Michael	Ducal Brittany 1364–1399
8271484	KNOX & PELCZYNSKI	Hegel's Political Writings
8225253	LE PATOUREL John	The Norman Empire
8212720	LENNARD Reginald	Rural England 1086–1135
8212321	LEVISON W.	England and the Continent in the 8th century
8148224	LIEBESCHUETZ J.H.W.G.	Continuity and Change in Roman Religion
8141378	LOBEL Edgar & PAGE Sir Denys	Poetarum Lesbiorum Fragmenta
8152442	MAAS P. & TRYPANIS C.A .	Sancti Romani Melodi Cantica
8148178	MATTHEWS John	Western Aristocracies and Imperial Court AD 364–425
8223447	McFARLANE K.B.	Lancastrian Kings and Lollard Knights
8226578	McFARLANE K.B.	The Nobility of Later Medieval England
8148100	MEIGGS Russell	Roman Ostia
8148402	MEIGGS Russell	Trees and Timber in the Ancient Mediterranean World
8142641	MILLER J. Innes	The Spice Trade of the Roman Empire
8147813	MOORHEAD John	Theodoric in Italy
8264259	MOORMAN John	A History of the Franciscan Order
8116020	OWEN A.L.	The Famous Druids
8143427	PFEIFFER R.	History of Classical Scholarship (vol 1)
8111649	PHEIFER J.D.	Old English Glosses in the Epinal-Erfurt Glossary
8142277	PICKARD–CAMBRIDGE A.W.	Dithyramb Tragedy and Comedy
8269765	PLATER & WHITE	Grammar of the Vulgate
8213891	PLUMMER Charles	Lives of Irish Saints (2 vols)
820695X	POWICKE Michael	Military Obligation in Medieval England
8269684	POWICKE Sir Maurice	Stephen Langton
821460X	POWICKE Sir Maurice	The Christian Life in the Middle Ages
8225369	PRAWER Joshua	Crusader Institutions
8225571	PRAWER Joshua	The History of The Jews in the Latin Kingdom of Jerusalem
8143249	RABY F.J.E.	A History of Christian Latin Poetry
8143257	RABY F.J.E.	A History of Secular Latin Poetry in the Middle Ages (2 vols)
8214316	RASHDALL & POWICKE	The Universities of Europe in the Middle Ages (3 vols)
8148380	RICKMAN Geoffrey	The Corn Supply of Ancient Rome
8141076	ROSS Sir David	Aristotle: Metaphysics (2 vols)
8141092	ROSS Sir David	Aristotle: Physics
8264178	RUNCIMAN Sir Steven	The Eastern Schism
814833X	SALMON J.B.	Wealthy Corinth
8171587	SALZMAN L.F.	Building in England Down to 1540
8218362	SAYERS Jane E.	Papal Judges Delegate in the Province of Canterbury 1198–1254
8221657	SCHEIN Sylvia	Fideles Crucis
8148135	SHERWIN WHITE A.N.	The Roman Citizenship
8642040	SOUTER Alexander	A Glossary of Later Latin to 600 AD
8222254	SOUTHERN R.W.	Eadmer: Life of St. Anselm
8251408	SQUIBB G.	The High Court of Chivalry
8212011	STEVENSON & WHITELOCK	Asser's Life of King Alfred
8212011	SWEET Henry	A Second Anglo-Saxon Reader—Archaic and Dialectical
8148259	SYME Sir Ronald	History in Ovid

8143273	SYME Sir Ronald	Tacitus (2 vols)
8200951	THOMPSON Sally	Women Religious
8201745	WALKER Simon	The Lancastrian Affinity 1361–1399
8161115	WELLESZ Egon	A History of Byzantine Music and Hymnography
8140185	WEST M.L.	Greek Metre
8141696	WEST M.L.	Hesiod: Theogony
8148542	WEST M.L.	The Orphic Poems
8140053	WEST M.L.	Hesiod: Works & Days
822799X	WHITBY M. & M.	The History of Theophylact Simocatta
8114877	WOOLF Rosemary	The English Religious Lyric in the Middle Ages
8119224	WRIGHT Joseph	Grammar of the Gothic Language